BIG ENGLISH 4

Mario Herrera • Christopher Sol Cruz

Contents

1 Kids in My Class 2
2 Our Schedule 14
3 I Like to Eat! 26
Checkpoint Units 1–3 38

4 How Do you Feel? 42
5 Weird and Wild Animals 54
6 Life Long Ago 66
Checkpoint Units 4–6 78

7 Special Days 82
8 Hobbies 94
9 Learning New Things 106
Checkpoint Units 7–9 118

Checkpoint Cutouts 123
YLE Practice Materials 129
Stickers

BIG ENGLISH Song

From the mountaintops to the bottom of the sea,
From a big blue whale to a baby bumblebee—
If you're big, if you're small, you can have it all,
And you can be anything you want to be!

It's bigger than you. It's bigger than me.
There's so much to do, and there's so much to see!
The world is big and beautiful, and so are we!
Think big! Dream big! Big English!

So in every land, from the desert to the sea,
We can all join hands and be one big family.
If we love, if we care, we can go anywhere!
The world belongs to everyone; it's ours to share.

It's bigger than you. It's bigger than me.
There's so much to do, and there's so much to see!
The world is big and beautiful, and so are we!
Think big! Dream big! Big English!

It's bigger than you. It's bigger than me.
There's so much to do, and there's so much to see!
The world is big and beautiful and waiting for me . . .
a one, two, three . . .
Think big! Dream big! Big English!

unit 1 Kids in My CLASS

A3 **1** **Listen and read. Then sing.**

Who's That Girl?

It's the first day of school,
We're back in our classes.
Everybody looks different—
And I have new glasses!

Who's that girl
Standing over there?
She's taller than me
And has dark curly hair.

In my class are the kids I know.
We all change. We all grow.

Wait, I know her.
That's Brenda. She's great!
Last year she was shorter,
And her hair was straight.

We're all getting bigger
Than we were last year.
But some things won't change
Like the friends we make here.

(Chorus)

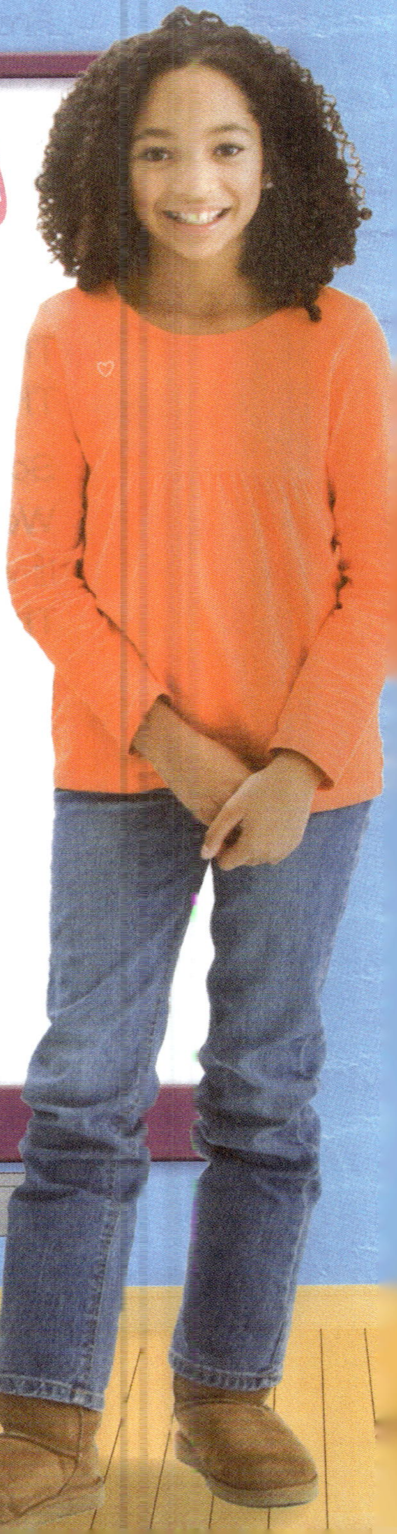

A4

2 Listen. Number the pictures from 1–6.

Trish is **tall** and has **long light brown** hair. She plays the flute.

Darren is **short**. He has **straight black** hair and glasses. He's **shy**.

Sylvia has **brown** hair. She carries a **bright pink** backpack.

Natalie has **wavy blonde** hair. She's **smart** and likes to read.

Bryan has **dark brown** hair and glasses. He's **serious**.

Larry has **light brown** hair. He's **friendly** and **funny**.

3 Circle *T* for *true* or *F* for *false*. Then check your answers with a partner.

	True	False
1. Sylvia has brown hair.	T	F
2. Natalie wears glasses.	T	F
3. Larry is shy.	T	F
4. Bryan is serious.	T	F
5. Trish plays the saxophone.	T	F
6. Darren is tall.	T	F

A5

4 THINK BIG Work with a partner. Listen. Talk about the people in 2.

What's Trish like?

She's tall and has long light brown hair.

A6–7

5 **Listen and read.**

She's Just Like You!

1 Cristina tells her dad about a new student at school.

2 Cristina and the new girl have some things in common.

3 But Cristina and Amanda are different in some ways, too.

4 Cristina likes her new classmate.

5 Cristina's dad makes a joke.

6 Cristina is definitely not shy!

READING COMPREHENSION

6 Read. Circle *same* or *different*.

	Cristina and Amanda	
1. She has dark curly hair.	same	different
2. Her hair is long.	same	different
3. She is nice and smart.	same	different
4. She is shy.	same	different

7 THINK BIG Talk about the questions with a partner.

1. How are you the same as Cristina or Amanda? Explain.
2. How are you different from Cristina or Amanda? Explain.
3. Are there times when you feel shy? Give an example.

A8

8 Listen and read. Say.

Lisa: Is that your cousin?

Marcy: Yes, that's Alan.

Lisa: Is he older than you?

Marcy: No, he's younger than me.

Lisa: Oh. He's taller than you.

Marcy: I know. He's taller than my brother David, too.

9 Practice the dialogue in 8 with a partner.

A9

10 Listen and stick.

Donna

Henry

Maddie

Joseph

Sandra

Who is **bigger**, Chris or Tom?	Chris is **bigger than** Tom.

old →	old**er**
big →	big**ger**
heavy →	heav**ier**

11 Look at the picture. Complete the sentences.

big heavy long small

1. Juan is bigger than Mia.
2. Mia is ________ than Juan.
3. Mia's hair is ________ than Juan's.
4. Juan's backpack is ________ than Mia's.

My sister's hair is longer than **my hair**.	My sister's hair is longer than **mine**.
My sister's hair is longer than **your hair**.	My sister's hair is longer than **yours**.

My sister's hair is longer than	**mine.**
	yours.
	his/hers.
	ours.
	theirs.

12 Rewrite the sentences.

his mine ours theirs yours

1. My sister is younger than **your sister**. My sister is younger than yours.
2. His book is heavier than **her book**. ________
3. Annette's hair is shorter than **my hair**. ________
4. Their car is bigger than **our car**. ________

13 THINK BIG Tell a partner about things in your class.

Shaun's backpack is heavier than mine.

CONTENT WORDS
chance common fraternal identical multiple birth pair

A10
14 **Listen and read.**

identical twins

Twins and More

One out of every 32 births is a pair of twins. Some twins are *identical*—they look exactly alike. Other twins are *fraternal*—they don't look alike.

When a mother gives birth to more than one baby at a time it is called a *multiple birth*. What we call each kind of multiple birth depends on the number of babies born. *Twins* (two babies) are the most common kind of multiple birth. *Triplets* (three babies), *quadruplets* (four babies), and larger groups are less common.

Number of Babies	Name of Birth Group	Rate
2	twins	1 out of 32 births
3	triplets	1 out of 625 births
4	quadruplets	1 out of 9,000 births

fraternal twins

Fraternal twins are more common than identical twins. In larger birth groups, identical babies are very rare. Some scientists say the chance of having all identical quadruplets is only 1 in 13 million!

Birth Group	Identical	Fraternal
twins	30%	70%
triplets	8%	92%
quadruplets	Less than 1%	More than 99%

15 **Look at the charts and answer the questions.**

1. Which are more common—identical twins or fraternal twins?
2. Which are more common—triplets or quadruplets?

16 **THINK BIG** **Work with a partner. Go to the library or use the Internet to find out more about multiple births. Share your information with the class.**

quadruplets

A11 17 Listen and read.

The World Beard and Moustache Championship

1

2

3

4

In the 1990s, a group of men in Germany started a competition comparing their beards and moustaches. Soon competitors came from other countries such as Switzerland, Norway, and the United States. They held the World Beard and Moustache Championship every two years. The contest has sixteen different categories, or types, of beards and moustaches.

The English Moustache is long and goes out to the sides. The Dalí Moustache, named after Spanish painter Salvador Dalí, is long and points up.

The Verdi category gets its name from Italian composer Giuseppe Verdi. This style has a straight beard and a curly moustache. The Freestyle Beard is really fun. Competitors in this category have beards of all different shapes and styles.

18 **Write the name of the category of each moustache or beard.**

1. ____________________ 3. ____________________

2. ____________________ 4. ____________________

19 THINK BIG **Work with a partner. Ask and answer.**

1. Which of the pictures is your favorite? Why?
2. Does anyone you know have a beard or a moustache? If so, who? Is the beard or moustache similar to one described in this article?

Writing | Parts of a Paragraph

A paragraph starts with a **topic sentence**. The topic sentence introduces the topic, or the main idea, of the paragraph.

My best friend's name is Gabe.

Detail sentences give details, or information, about the main idea. They come after the topic sentence.

He is taller than me and wears cool glasses.
Gabe is smart, and he is funny, too.
We like to play soccer together on weekends.

A paragraph ends with a **final sentence**. A final sentence talks about the subject again in a different way.

I'm happy to have a friend like Gabe.

20 **Read the sentences from a paragraph. Write *T* for *topic sentence*, *D* for *detail sentence*, or *F* for *final sentence*.**

_____ **1.** She is very nice and lots of fun.

_____ **2.** I'm always glad to see Aunt Elsie.

_____ **3.** She likes to make cookies with my sister and me.

_____ **4.** My favorite aunt is my Aunt Elsie.

_____ **5.** She likes to play games with us.

21 **Write a paragraph about a friend or a favorite relative. Share your paragraph with the class.**

____

(title)

____

____

____

____

____

____

____

Writing Steps

1. Think of a friend or a relative you like a lot.
2. Think about why you like this person.
3. Write a title.
4. Write a topic sentence.
5. Add detail sentences to give information about your subject.
6. Write a final sentence.

A12

22 **Listen and complete the sentences.**

dropped | first | help | turn

1. You can have a ______________.

2. Can I ______________ you?

3. You can go ______________.

4. You ______________ something.

23 **Practice being considerate with a partner.**

You can go first.

Thank you!

PROJECT

24 **Make Good Manners award ribbons. Your teacher can give them to students who are considerate and have good manners.**

Review | Listening and Speaking

25 **Work in a group. Make cards with these words on them.**

friendly	funny	glasses	hair	long
nice	old	short	tall	young

Place the cards face down. Take turns turning over a card. Say a sentence about one person in your group using the word on the card.

You get a point for each correct sentence. Play until everyone in your group has five points.

Vocabulary and Grammar | Review

26 **Complete the paragraph. Use the words from the box.**

blonde	brown	funny
glasses	serious	

My two friends are very different. My friend Martin is ______________. He has short ______________ hair, and he wears ______________. My friend Millie is ______________. She has long ______________ hair. Martin and Millie are both nice. I like my friends!

27 **Complete the dialogue. Use the words from the box.**

he	him	older	short
shorter	taller	you	yours

A: Is that your brother?

B: Yes, that's Max.

A: Is he ______________ than ______________?

B: Yes. I'm 10, and he's 11. But I'm a little ______________ than ______________.

A: His hair is ______________ than ______________.

B: Yes. I don't really like ______________ hair.

A: Is he friendly?

B: Yes, ______________ is very friendly. Just like me!

I Can

- ☐ **make comparisons.**
- ☐ **describe people.**

unit 2

Our SCHEDULE

A13 1 **Listen and read. Then sing.**

Things We Do

There are lots and lots of things
I want to do every day,
Like order pizza, watch a movie,
Stay up late, and play!

But there are lots of other things
I don't want to do so much,
Like set the table, wash the dishes,
Make my bed, and such.

Chores, chores—there's lots to do.
We do our chores. You should, too!

I take out the recycling
On Tuesdays before school.
And I feed and walk our dog,
But I don't mind—she's cool.

We all do our chores at home
Sometimes twice a day.
We all help our families
In lots of different ways.

(Chorus)

A14

2 **Read, listen, and write.**

afternoon
once
Saturday
summer
three times
twice
week

1. I help clean every ____________.

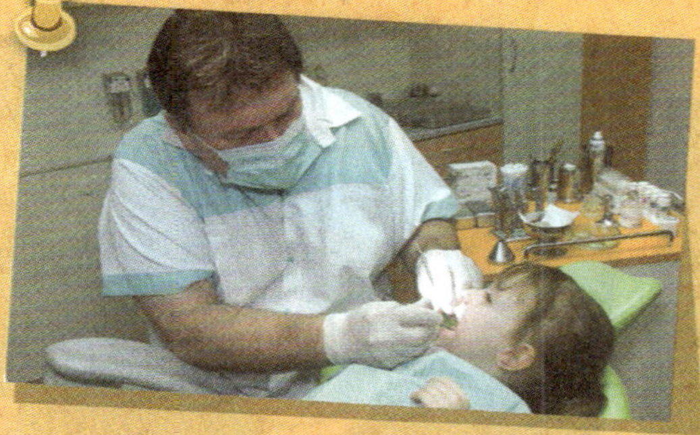

2. I go to the dentist ____________ a year.

3. We go on vacation every ____________.

4. We watch a movie once a ____________.

5. We shop for food ____________ a week.

6. My parents eat out ____________ a month.

7. We play outside every ____________.

3 THINK BIG **Complete the sentences. Then share your work with a partner.**

1. Every Saturday I ____________.
2. Every morning I ____________.
3. I ____________ once a week.
4. I ____________ twice a year.

Every Saturday I clean my room.

Every morning I take out the garbage.

4 Listen and read. A15–16

5 Kim has a lot of cousins.

6 Kim is thinking about all the dresses she has to wear to her cousins' weddings.

READING COMPREHENSION

5 Circle *T* for *true* and *F* for *false*.

	True	False
1. Kim likes to go to weddings.	T	F
2. Kim likes to wear dresses.	T	F
3. Kim has a lot of cousins.	T	F
4. All of Kim's cousins are older than she is.	T	F
5. All of Kim's cousins are getting married this year.	T	F

6 THINK BIG Ask and answer with a partner.

1. Do you like to go to weddings? Why or why not?
2. On what special days do you dress up?
3. Do you enjoy dressing up? Why or why not?

Language in Action

A17 **7** **Listen and read. Say.**

Logan: Oh, no! It's Tuesday.

Brian: What's the matter?

Logan: I have a guitar lesson today. I don't really like guitar lessons.

Brian: How often do you have them?

Logan: Twice a week, on Tuesdays and Thursdays.

Brian: Hey, I have an idea. Let's trade schedules.

Logan: Why? What are you doing today?

Brian: I'm going to the dentist.

Logan: Uh, no thanks!

8 **Practice the dialogue in 7 with a partner.**

A18 **9** **Listen and stick. Number the pictures.**

____

____

____

____

Where is	he/she	going after school?	He/She	is going to soccer practice.
What are	you	doing tonight?	I	am watching a movie at home.
			We	are watching a movie at home.
	they		They	

10 Complete the questions. Then match questions and answers.

b 1. What are they doing after school?

___ 2. ___ is your sister going?

___ 3. ___ are we going after dinner?

___ 4. ___ is Mr. Lee doing after class?

a. She's going to the library.

b. They're going shopping.

c. He's helping in the school garden.

d. We're going to Grandma's house.

How often does	he/she	have guitar lessons?	Once a week. Twice a year. Every Friday. On Sundays. Once a month. Every summer.
How often do	you	go to the dentist?	
	they		

11 Answer the questions.

1. How often do you go to the dentist?

___

2. How often do you play sports?

___

3. How often does your English teacher give tests?

___

4. How often does your best friend come to your home?

___

12 THINK BIG Work with a partner. Ask and answer questions about the activities on pages 14–15.

activities on pages 14–15

How often do you clean your room?

I clean my room every weekend.

CONTENT WORDS

ad attractive believe popular remember tool

A19 13 **Listen and read.**

Advertising

Companies spend a lot of money on advertising. Advertisements, or ads, are everywhere. They are all around you! Here are some places you can find ads:

Companies want you to buy things. That's the job of advertising. What kinds of tools do advertisers use? They use tools such as these:

Characters: a cartoon character on a box of cereal

Famous People: a basketball player selling athletic shoes

Slogans and Jingles: words and tunes that you remember all day

Design: bright colors and interesting images to catch your eye

Many companies try to sell things to kids. Do you believe ads? Be careful! Advertisers know what you like. They try to make you think that their product can do these things for you:

- make you happier.
- make you more popular.
- make you look more attractive.
- make you look older or younger.

14 THINK BIG **Find an advertisement. Answer the questions.**

1. Who is this ad for? Kids, adults, or teens?
2. What tools does this ad use?
3. Do you believe what the ad says? Why or why not?

15 **Work with a partner. Present an ad to your class.**

This car ad uses a cool design and a catchy slogan.

A20

16 **Listen and read.**

UNUSUAL Habits

People all over the globe have unusual habits. Here is a page from a website that explores this secret world.

What unusual habits do you have?

	**birdsong** 11:38 a.m. reply	I live in Libya, Africa. It's REALLY hot all the time. So I take a shower three times a day. I know, it's a lot. But it cools me off, and I like to feel clean!
	**racerXYZ** 11:40 a.m. reply	I have a strange habit. I never touch doorknobs. Sometimes I'm stuck in a room, and I wait for someone to enter or leave to help me get out. I really like sliding doors because they don't have doorknobs. Lucky for me that I live in Tokyo, Japan. We have lots of sliding doors here.
	**snowflake** 11:43 a.m. reply	My habits aren't really unusual. Well, there's one. I drink milk twice a day. But always WITH ICE. I can drink only really COLD milk. Our milk here in Hertfordshire, England, is delicious.
	**hatman22** 11:44 a.m. reply	I wear a hat every day. I wear it to school. I wear it to bed. I even wear it in the shower! I guess that's pretty strange. But it's cold where I live–in Rio Grande, Argentina.
	**ABC_girl** 11:49 a.m. reply	You guys don't have strange habits. Listen to this! I always put the books on my bookshelf in alphabetical order. I check them every morning. If one is in the wrong place, I fix it.
	**tbear02** 11:57 a.m. reply	I'm a little like you, ABC_girl. I make my bed every morning. Then I put all my stuffed animals on the bed. The animals have to be in the same place every day.

17 **THINK BIG** **Ask and answer with a partner.**

1. Which of these habits do you think are unusual? Why?
2. Does anyone in your family have any unusual habits? Explain.
3. Do you think it's easy for people to write about their unusual habits on a website like this? Why or why not?

Writing | Using Sequence Words

Sequence words tell the order in which things happen. Here are some examples:

My Day at School

First, we have a math lesson.
Next, we have a spelling test.
Then we have lunch.
After that, we have a social studies lesson.
Finally, we have a reading lesson.

Use *first* for the first activity. Use *finally* for the last activity. For the activities in between, you can use the sequence words in any order.

18 **Underline the sequence words in the paragraph.**

My family and I go to the beach on Saturdays in the summer. First, we go swimming in the ocean. Next, we have a picnic under a big umbrella. After that, my mom and dad read, and my brothers and I go swimming again. Then we get in the car to go home. Finally, we stop for ice cream!

19 **Write a list of things you do on Saturdays. Then number them in the correct order.**

What I Do on Saturdays

20 **In your notebook, write a paragraph about what you do on Saturdays. Use sequence words. Share your paragraph with the class.**

Practice good habits. | Values in Action

A2 21 **Listen and read. Circle the happy face for good habits or the sad face for bad habits.**

1. I make my bed every day. ☺ ☹

2. I eat vegetables only once a week. ☺ ☹

3. I do my homework and watch movies at the same time. ☺ ☹

4. I help do the dishes every day. ☺ ☹

22 **Talk about your habits with a partner.**

I exercise three times a week.

That's a good habit!

PROJECT

23 **Work with your classmates to make a Good Habits mural. Hang it on a wall in your school.**

24 Form groups to play the *Silly Sentences* game. First, work with your group to write activities such as *practice the piano* and *make my bed* on ten cards. Then write expressions of frequency (*on Tuesdays*, *every day*, and so on) on ten cards.

Next, play the game. Taking turns, turn over one card from each stack and make a silly sentence.

Finally, tell the class some silly sentences from your group. Then tell how you would correct each sentence.

25 Complete the dialogues. Write answers using the pictures.

1\.

A: What do you do before school?

B: I take out the garbage.

2\.

A: What do you do after school?

B: ______________________

3\.

A: What do you do on weekends?

B: ______________________

4\.

A: What are you doing this summer?

B: I'm going on vacation.

5\.

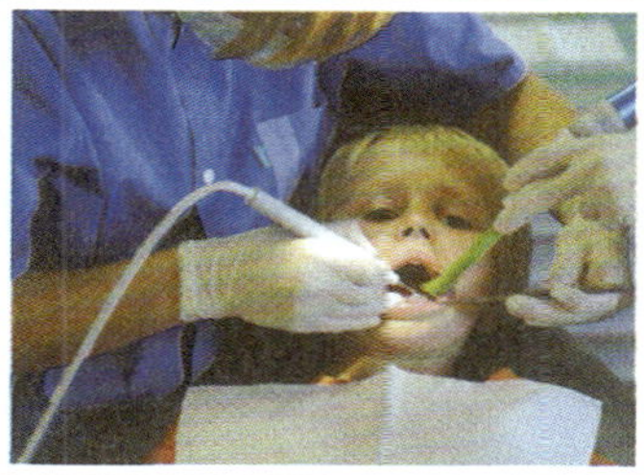

A: Where are you going after class?

B: ______________________

6\.

A: What are you doing this afternoon?

B: ______________________

26 Circle the correct word in each pair.

A: How **often** / **many** do you visit your grandparents?

B: We see them **once** / **times** a week. We go **on** / **every** weekend.

A: That's nice. My grandma **always** / **twice** makes a big pie. It's delicious!

B: Cool. I see my grandparents only **once** / **sometimes** a year.

I Can

- ☐ talk about what people are doing at different times.
- ☐ talk about where people are going at different times.
- ☐ say how often people do things.

unit 3 I Like to EAT!

A22 1 **Listen and read. Then sing.**

Try Something New

"Hey there, Sam, try something new.
Just take a little bite and chew.
Now's your chance. Please don't waste it.
You won't know if you like it till you taste it."

"Would you like some beef fried rice?
Tonight it tastes especially nice!"
Sam says, "No, Dad, not right now.
But thanks so much—thanks, anyhow."

Come on, Sam, please take a little taste!
Come on, Sam, don't make a funny face!

"How about a sweet steamed bun?
It's really yummy. Come on, try one!"
Sam says, "No, Dad, not right now.
But thanks so much—thanks, anyhow."

"Would you like some chicken curry?"
"No thanks, Dad. I'm in a hurry!"
"How about a corn tortilla?"
"No thanks, Dad. Later! See ya!"

(Chorus)

"Come on, Sam. Just one little bite!"
"Oh my gosh, Dad. Oh, All right!
Mmm. Hey, you're right. It's great!
Please put some more on my plate!"

1. steamed buns

2. chicken curry

A23

2 Listen. Point and say.

3. oatmeal

4. eggs in tortillas

5. cereal with milk

6. yogurt with fruit

7. rice and beans

8. noodle soup

9. pasta with vegetables

10. grilled cheese sandwich

A24

3 Listen and write the numbers of the foods from 2.

______ Isabella
Italy

______ Mei Lin
China

______ Oliver
Scotland

______ Angela
Mexico

______ Alan
United States

4 THINK BIG Work with a partner. Ask and answer.

1. Which child's meals do you like? Which do you not like?
2. What do you like to eat for breakfast? For lunch?
3. What can you say about the foods people in different places eat?

A25–26 5 **Listen and read.**

Homemade Lemonade

1 Theo makes some fresh lemonade.

2 Patty can't drink the lemonade. It's too sour! She spits it out.

3 Theo wants to give Patty some more lemonade.

4 Theo's happy—he thinks Patty likes his lemonade.

5 Patty doesn't want to tell Theo that she doesn't like his lemonade.

6 Theo figures out why Patty doesn't want more lemonade.

READING COMPREHENSION

lemonade	more	sour	sugar	thinks

6 Read and complete the summary.

Theo makes some ____________. Patty tries it, but it's too ____________. Theo thinks Patty likes it, so he gives her ____________. Then Theo ____________ about how he made the lemonade. He forgot to put ____________ in it! That's why it's sour.

7 THINK BIG Ask and answer with a partner.

1. Why doesn't Patty tell Theo his lemonade is sour?
2. Why does Theo give Patty a second glass of lemonade?
3. If you try a food or drink that you don't like, what do you do?

Language in Action

A27

8 **Listen and read. Say.**

Grandpa: What would you like for lunch, Aiden?
Aiden: I'd like a sandwich, please.
Grandpa: I'm making a BLT. Would you like one?
Aiden: What's a BLT?
Grandpa: Bacon, lettuce, and tomato—on toast.
Aiden: That sounds great! May I have two?
Grandpa: Two sandwiches? You must be hungry! Would you like some milk, too?
Aiden: Yes, I would. Thanks, Grandpa.

9 **Practice the dialogue in 8 with a partner.**

A28

10 **Listen and stick. Write a word from the box next to each picture.**

salty   sour   spicy   sweet

1.

green mango smoothie ______________

2.

blue corn tortilla chips ______________

3.

chili ______________

4.

flan ______________

What **would** you **like**?			I'**d like** some soup.		I would like → I'd like
What **would**	he/she	**like?**	He'**d**/She'**d**	**like** yogurt.	He/She would like → He'd/She'd like

11 Look and complete.

1. What _would_ Jessie _like_? _She'd like_ some oatmeal.
2. What ________ Jin-Soo ________? ________ some noodle soup.

3. What ________ Ms. Ruiz ________? ________ yogurt and fruit.
4. What ________ you ________? ________________.

Would	you	**like to try** some curry?	**Yes,**	I	**would.**	**No,**	I	**wouldn't.**
	he/she			we			we	
	they			he/she			he/she	
				they			they	

12 Read and complete.

1. Would your dad like to try a steamed bun? Yes, ________________.
2. Would your mom like to try some flan? No, ________________.
3. Would you like to try a berry smoothie? ________________.
4. ________________________________? Yes, I would.

CONTENT WORDS
balanced dairy diet grains guide protein

A29
13 **Listen and read.**

A Balanced Diet

For a balanced diet, eat foods from each of the five food groups every day: grains, vegetables, fruits, protein, and dairy. But how much of each food group should you have?

The chart below is called My Plate. It shows which foods to eat more of and which to eat less of. The Vegetables section is bigger than the Protein section. This means you should eat more vegetables than protein. Likewise, the Grains section is bigger than the Fruits section, so eat more grains than fruits. The Dairy section is smaller than the others, so eat fewer dairy foods than any other.

For a healthy body and mind, use the My Plate chart as a guide when you eat and follow these simple rules:

My Plate

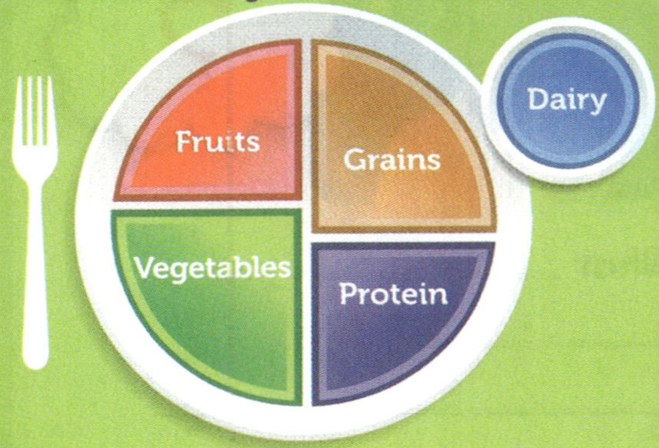

- **Eat foods you like, but don't eat too much.**
- **Fruits and vegetables should make up about half of what you eat.**
- **At least half of your grains should be whole grains.**
- **Drink fat-free or low-fat milk instead of whole milk.**
- **Stay away from foods that are too salty.**
- **Drink water instead of drinks that have sugar in them.**

14 **Write three foods for each of these food groups.**

1. Grains: ______________________
2. Vegetables: ______________________
3. Fruits: ______________________
4. Protein: ______________________
5. Dairy: ______________________

15 THINK BIG **What do you eat every day? Draw a My Plate chart for your eating habits. Then compare it with the chart on this page.**

A30 16 **Listen and read.**

School Lunches

Every day, kids all over the world eat lunch at school. Some kids bring their lunch from home. But many kids get their lunch from the school cafeteria. School lunches are different in different parts of the world.

Japan In Japan, kids eat lunch in their classroom. Students clear their desks. Then four or five students take turns serving the food each day. Rice and soup are often part of school lunches in Japan.

Brazil School lunch in Brazil is usually a meal with a balance of meat or fish, fruit and vegetables, and some bread. However, the main part of the meal is almost always rice and beans. Brazilian school lunches are healthy and filling. For most people in Brazil, lunch is bigger than breakfast or dinner.

Zambia In Zambia, many kids eat a dish called *nshima* for lunch. In fact, people in Zambia often eat nshima for both lunch and dinner. Nshima is a sticky dough made from white cornmeal. People eat nshima with their hands. They dip it into tasty sauces and usually eat it with some meat or fish.

Italy In Italy, the food in school lunches is organic, or grown naturally, without chemicals. The food also comes from farms near the school. These lunches usually include pasta or a rice dish called *risotto*. Kids eat salad for lunch, too. Most schools in Italy serve meat only a few times each week.

17 THINK BIG **Work with a partner. Ask and answer.**

1. What do you usually eat for lunch at school? Compare your lunch with your partner's.
2. Would you like to try any of the foods from this unit? Why or why not?
3. What is your favorite school lunch? Explain.

Writing | Conjunctions: *and*, *but*, *or*

Use conjunctions such as *and*, *but*, and *or* to join two sentences into one sentence.

I eat breakfast at home. Then I walk to school.
→ I eat breakfast at home, and then I walk to school.

Dad eats a big breakfast. Mom has only toast.
→ Dad eats a big breakfast, but Mom has only toast.

We can eat dinner at home. We can go to a restaurant.
→ We can eat dinner at home, or we can go to a restaurant.

18 Underline the conjunctions in the paragraph.

I like to eat vegetables, and I eat them every day. I like to drink fruit juice, but I don't really like to eat fruit. I can eat fruit with yogurt, or I can drink it in a smoothie. Sometimes I try to eat fruit by itself, but it always feels strange to me. I keep trying to eat fruit, and maybe someday I'll like it.

19 Join the sentences. Use the conjunction in parentheses.

1. My sister likes chicken curry. My brother likes steamed buns. (*and*)

   ____

2. I usually eat oatmeal in the morning. Today I had yogurt. (*but*)

   ____

3. We can have Mexican food. We can try the French restaurant. (*or*)

   ____

4. Dad makes soup on Sundays. Then he eats it every day for lunch. (*and*)

   ____

20 In your notebook, write three sentences about foods you like or don't like. Use each conjunction once.

A31

21 **Listen and complete. Use words from the box.**

apple	cake	carrots	chips	cookies	donuts	popcorn	yogurt

1. I like ____________, but ____________ is healthier.

2. ____________ are delicious, but they have a lot of sugar. I'll have an ____________.

3. I love ____________, but they're not really good for me. ____________ is better.

4. I had some ____________ last night. Today I want to have some ____________ for a snack.

22 **Talk about choosing healthy foods with a partner.**

I like candy, but a banana is healthier.

I like ice cream, but an orange is better.

PROJECT

23 **Make a Healthy Foods collage. Display it in your classroom.**

24 **Make your own restaurant. First, make a menu for breakfast and lunch.**

Rosie's Restaurant

Breakfast	
eggs and toast	$3.00
yogurt and fruit	$3.50
cereal with milk	$2.75
oatmeal	$2.75
orange juice	$2.00
milk	$1.75

Lunch	
noodle soup	$3.50
chicken curry	$5.25
pasta and vegetables	$4.95
grilled cheese sandwich	$4.50
fried rice	$3.75
lemonade	$2.00

Next, take food orders from your classmates. Write the orders.

What would you like for breakfast?

Would you like some milk with that?

I'd like some oatmeal, please.

Yes, I would. Thank you.

Name:	Name:	Name:
Breakfast:	Breakfast:	Breakfast:
Lunch:	Lunch:	Lunch:

Finally, tell the class what your classmates would like to have.

For breakfast, Manuela would like oatmeal with milk.

do (x2) like (x3) would (x3)

25 Complete the dialogue.

A: What ____________ you ____________ to eat for lunch?

B: I'm not sure.

A: ____________ you ____________ to go to the new Thai restaurant?

B: Yes, I ____________. What's Thai food like?

A: Some of it is spicy. ____________ you ____________ spicy food?

B: Yes, I ____________!

A: Great. Let's go.

26 Write the names.

1. ____________

2. ____________

3. ____________

4. ____________

5. ____________

6. ____________

27 Answer the questions. Write sentences.

1. What do you like to eat for breakfast?

   ____

2. What do you like to eat for lunch?

   ____

3. What do you like to eat for a snack?

   ____

I Can

☐ talk about what people eat.

☐ make polite requests.

How Well Do I Know It? Can I Use It?

1 **Read and circle.**

I know this. I need more practice. I don't know this.

	PAGES			
Describing people: friendly, has dark brown hair, serious, smart, tall, wears glasses . . .	2–3			
Activities: go to the dentist, help clean, shop for food, take out the recycling, walk the dog, watch a movie . . .	14–15			
Expressions of frequency: every Wednesday, once a week, three times a year . . .	15, 19			
Foods: oatmeal, noodle soup, rice and beans, tortillas . . .	26–27			
Tastes: sweet, sour, spicy, salty . . .	30			
Who is **bigger?** Chris is **bigger** than Tom. My sister's hair is longer than **my hair.** My sister's hair is longer than **mine.**	6–7			
What are you doing on Friday? We're going to the movies. **How often** do you go to the movies? We go to the movies once a week.	18–19			
What **would** you **like**? I'**d like** some oatmeal. **Would** she **like to try** some chicken curry? **Yes,** she **would**. / **No,** she **wouldn't**.	30–31			

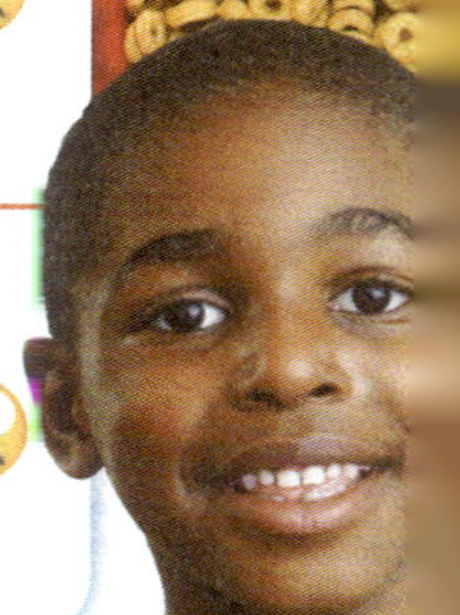

I Can Do It!

A32

2 Get ready.

A. Complete the dialogue. Write the numbers. Then listen and check.

1. Ms. Hart's hair is shorter than Ms. Roberts'.
2. She's really nice.
3. Ms. Hart is bringing pizza to class.
4. Ms. Hart brought some Indian vegetable curry to class.
5. Every Tuesday and Thursday.

Anna: We have a new social studies teacher. Her name is Ms. Hart.

Dad: What is she like?

Anna: _____. And she's funny, too!

Dad: Oh, I think I saw her. Does she have long blonde hair?

Anna: No, that's Ms. Roberts. _____ And Ms. Hart wears glasses.

Dad: Interesting. When do you have social studies?

Anna: _____. Right now we're learning about India. _____.

Dad: Really? Was it spicy?

Anna: Yeah. I loved it! Yesterday we learned about Spain, and Ms. Hart brought us hot chocolate and churros. Today we're learning about Italy. _____.

Dad: Stop. You're making me hungry!

B. Practice the dialogue in **A** with a partner.

C. Ask and answer the questions with a partner.

1. Would you like to try the foods in **A**?

2. What countries do you learn about in social studies?

3 Get set.

STEP 1 Create information about someone you would like to have as a pen pal. What is he/she like? Where does he/she live?

STEP 2 Cut out the book outline on page 123. Fold it to make a book.

STEP 3 Write about your pen pal in your book. Now you're ready to **GO!**

4 Go!

A. Trade books with three classmates. Write notes about their pen pals. Ask and answer questions like the ones below. Draw lines to places on the map where the pen pals live.

- What are the pen pals' names?
- What are they like?
- What do they like to do?
- What foods do they like to eat?

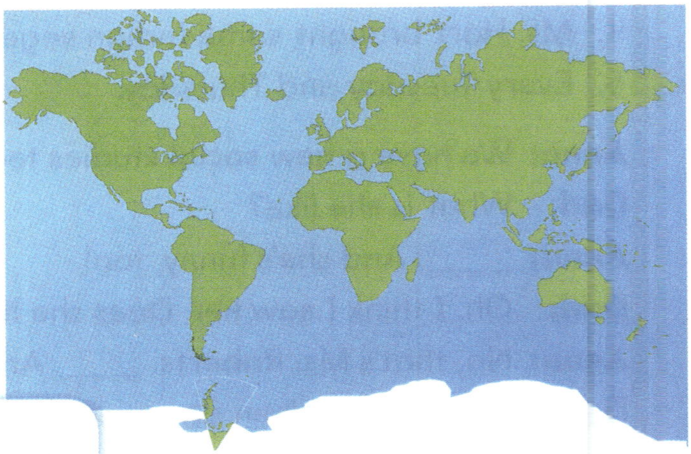

______________'s Pen Pal

____

____

____

______________'s Pen Pal

____

____

____

______________'s Pen Pal

____

____

____

B. Tell your classmates about some of your partners' pen pals.

Maria's pen pal lives in Taiwan. She likes to watch movies. She likes to eat pineapple cake!

5 Write about yourself.

- Who is taller, you or your best friend?
- What is your best friend like?
- What does your best friend look like?
- What do you like to do after school?
- How often do you play with your friends?
- What foods would you like to try?

All About Me

Date: ______________

____

____

____

____

____

____

How Well Do I Know It Now?

6 Read and circle.

A. **Go to page 38. Read and circle again. Use a different color.**

B. **Check (✔).**

☐ I can start the next unit.

☐ I can ask my teacher for help and then start the next unit.

☐ I can practice and then start the next unit.

7 Rate this Checkpoint. Check the boxes.

☐	☐	☐	☐	☐	☐	☐
very easy	easy	hard	very hard	fun	OK	not fun

unit 4 How Do You FEEL?

A33 1 **Listen and read. Then sing.**

Stay in Bed and Rest!

You're coughing, and you're sneezing.
You need to stay in bed.
I think you have a fever.
Here, let me feel your head.
You shouldn't go to school today.
You should stay home instead.

When you're sick or feeling blue,
Your family takes good care of you.

You have a fever and a cold.
Here's what I suggest:
You should drink some tea and juice.
Stay in bed and rest!
Listen to your dad now
Because your dad knows best.

(Chorus)

A34

2 Listen and say.

1. allergies
2. coughing
3. fever
4. headache
5. scrape
6. sneezing
7. sore throat
8. stomachache

A35

3 Listen and write the words from 2.

1. It's spring, and the flowers are starting to bloom. Pablo has terrible ____________________. He is ____________________, and his eyes are watering.

2. Sandra has a bad ____________________. She is ____________________, and she has a ____________________. She has to stay home from school.

3. Liz has an awful ____________________. She wants to close her eyes and rest.

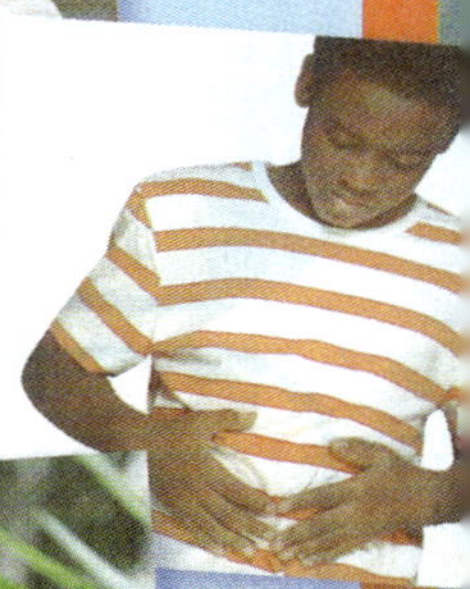

4. Ben has a bad ____________________. He ate something bad last night, and now he feels sick.

5. Cary fell and hurt himself on the playground. He has a big ____________________ on his knee.

4 THINK BIG Why are the people in 3 sad? Write the names and tell a partner.

1. ____________________ is sad because he can't eat anything right now.
2. ____________________ is sad because she can't go to school or see her friends.
3. ____________________ is sad because he can't play outside.
4. ____________________ is sad because his leg hurts.
5. ____________________ is sad because she can't study or watch TV.

Story

A36–37

5 **Listen and read.**

You Hurt Yourself!

1 Emma and Paul are eating lunch together at school. Emma has a problem.

2 Paul gets upset when he sees Emma's arm.

3 Paul wants to help Emma.

4 Emma doesn't need to go to the nurse. She's all right.

5 Emma cleans off her arm.

6 Now Paul doesn't feel so well!

READING COMPREHENSION

6 **Who says it? Write *P* for *Paul* or *E* for *Emma*.**

_____ **1.** You should see the school nurse!

_____ **2.** I just need a napkin.

_____ **3.** You cut yourself!

_____ **4.** I don't need a nurse.

_____ **5.** It's only ketchup.

_____ **6.** You shouldn't wait!

7 THINK BIG **Ask and answer with a partner.**

1. Why did Paul get upset?
2. Why didn't Emma get upset?
3. What do you do when you get hurt?

Language in Action

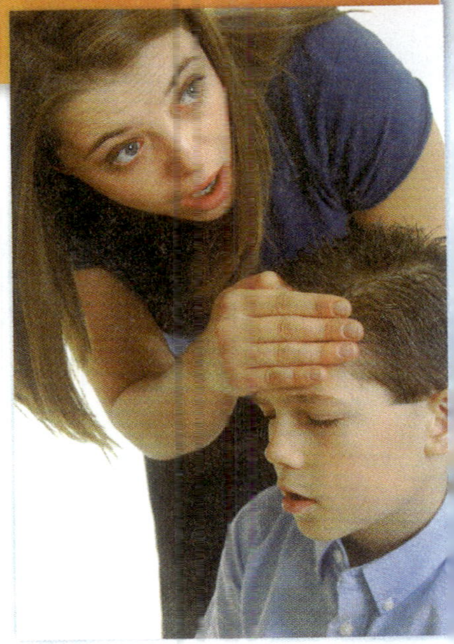

A38

8 **Listen and read. Say.**

Mom: What's the matter?

Jacob: I don't know. I feel kind of sick.

Mom: Let me see. Wow. Your forehead is warm. You have a fever.

Jacob: Really?

Mom: Yes. You should take some medicine and get some rest.

Jacob: But . . . what about my soccer game today?

Mom: You can watch a soccer game on TV.

9 **Practice the dialogue in 8 with a partner.**

A39

10 **Listen and stick. Write the number.**

____

He should get an X-ray.

____

She should see a dentist.

____

She should take some medicine.

____

He should eat soup and go to bed.

I	**should** eat healthy foods.	I	**shouldn't** stay up late.
You		You	
He/She		He/She	
We		We	
They		They	

11 **Complete the sentences with *should* or *shouldn't*.**

1. You ______________ get some exercise every day.
2. Sue ______________ eat so many sweets.
3. Children ______________ watch too much TV.
4. People ______________ drink lots of water and get plenty of rest.

I	should take care of	**myself.**
You		**yourself.**
He/She		**himself/herself.**
We		**ourselves.**
They		**themselves.**

12 **Read and complete.**

1. I eat too many sweets. I should take better care of ______________.
2. My sister often goes to bed late. She should take care of ______________.
3. My brother exercises every day. He takes good care of ______________.
4. My family grows vegetables in the garden. We eat good food and take care of ______________.
5. You should take care of ______________, too.
6. My grandparents are 80. They take good care of ______________.

13 **Work with a partner. Talk about the people on pages 42–43.**

He has a scrape.

He should see the school nurse.

CONTENT WORDS
bacteria fungi germs protozoa toxins viruses

A40
14 **Listen and read.**

Germs

Our bodies work hard to stay healthy. But there are many tiny enemies around us that can make us sick. These little enemies are called germs. There are four main types of germs: bacteria, viruses, fungi, and protozoa.

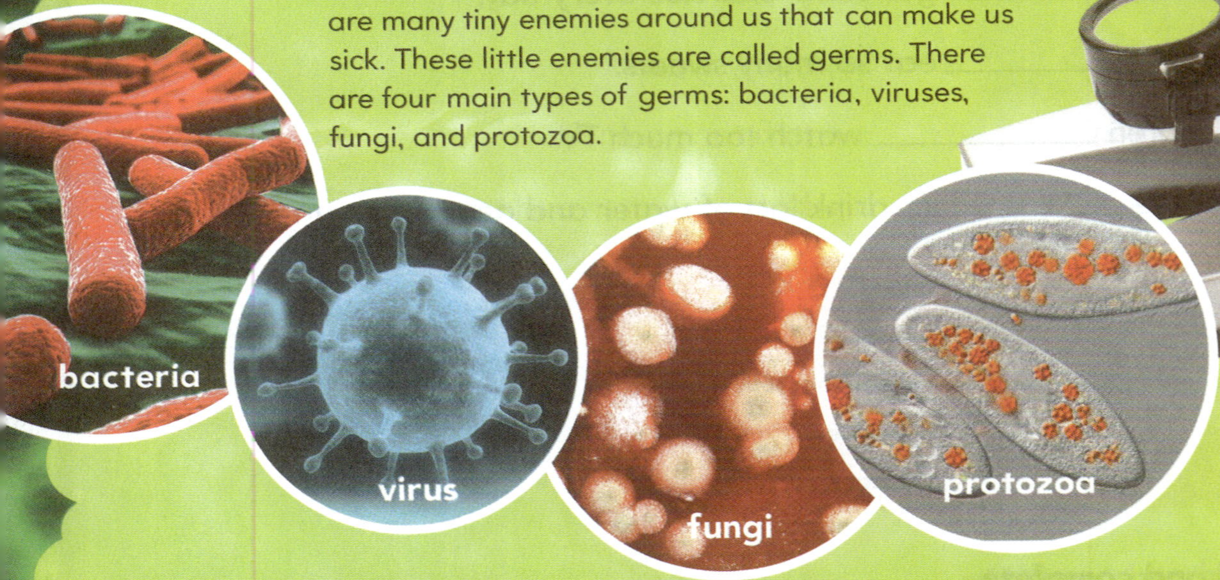

Germs in Your Body Germs are so small that we can see them only with a microscope. They come into our bodies, eat up the body's nutrients, and take away our energy. Many germs make a kind of poison called a toxin. Toxins can cause fever, coughing, or other ailments. It is important to stay away from germs as much as possible.

Germs in Your Home Germs are all around us. One of the easiest places to find them is at home. The clipboard shows five places in your home that are perfect for germs.

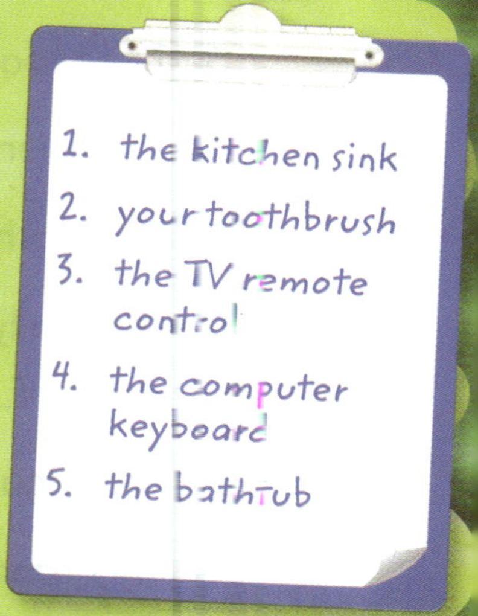

Protect Yourself Not all germs are bad. But we have to protect ourselves from dangerous germs. We can do this by washing our hands often and keeping our homes clean.

15 THINK BIG **Read and research with a partner. Discuss with the class.**

1. Why do you think the kitchen sink, the bathtub, and your toothbrush are easy places for germs to live?
2. What can we do protect ourselves from germs in those places?

A47

16 **Listen and read.**

Different Cultures, Different Remedies

Do you see a doctor every time you have a cold? Of course not. Your parents just take care of you at home. They use home remedies. Let's take a look at some popular home remedies used around the world.

Chicken Soup When the first signs of a cold begin, people in many countries make a big pot of hot chicken soup. They eat the soup and rest. Many people believe that chicken soup is a natural and healthy cure for a cold.

Boiled Eggs In China, it is common to rub a hot hard-boiled egg on your face, head, and neck to cure a headache. You boil the egg, take off the shell, and rub the egg on your head until the egg becomes cool. Many people believe this will help your headache and improve your sleep.

Vinegar People in many countries use vinegar as a medicine. For example, some people in Germany use vinegar to help with sunburn. They rub it onto the skin to make the pain go away. Some people in Russia rub vinegar on the skin to help with a fever.

Tea Many people around the world use tea, especially herbal tea, to cure common problems. Some ingredients in home remedy teas include ginger, garlic, honey, and lemon. Popular in Greece, Spain, Korea, Japan, and other countries, tea is one of the world's oldest home remedies.

17 THINK BIG **Work with a partner. Ask and answer.**

1. Have you ever tried one of these home remedies? Explain.
2. Do you think home remedies like these really work? Why or why not?
3. Does your family have any special home remedies? Describe them and what they do.

Writing | Using Commas

Use a comma before conjunctions such as *and*, *but*, and *or* when joining two sentences into one sentence.

I eat good food. I exercise every day.
→ I eat good food, and I exercise every day.

My sister likes sweets. She doesn't eat them every day.
→ My sister likes sweets, but she doesn't eat them every day.

We can take a walk in the park. We can watch some TV.
→ We can take a walk in the park, or we can watch some TV.

Use commas to separate items in a list.

I like walking in the park, riding my bicycle, listening to music, watching movies, and shopping.

18 **Put commas where they belong in the paragraph.**

I get up early every day and I ride my bike to school. I like school but sometimes I don't want to study. I know I should study after school but I often just want to play with my friends. What do you think? Should I do my homework or should I go out to play with my friends?

19 **In your notebook, make a list of things you like to do and things you don't like to do. Be sure to separate the things in your list with commas.**

Things I Like to Do	Things I Don't Like to Do
I like to talk to my friends, swim, read books, and cook.	I don't like to clean my room, go to the dentist, or take tests.

A42

20 **Listen and number in order.**

_____ You should cough or sneeze into the inside of your arm.

_____ You should wash your hands often.

_____ You shouldn't share food, cups, forks, or spoons.

21 **Tell a partner how you can stop spreading germs.**

PROJECT

22 **Make a Good Hygiene Habits checklist. Compare your checklist with a partner's.**

Name ______________________

Good Hygiene Habits

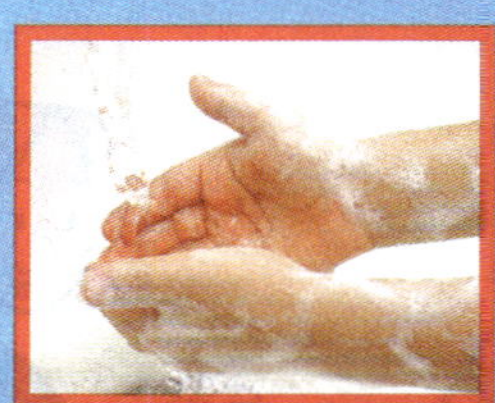

Wash your hands. ☐

Cough or sneeze into your arm. ☐

Don't share food, cups, forks, or spoons. ☐

23 Work with a partner. Make cards with the names of the different ailments you learned in this unit.

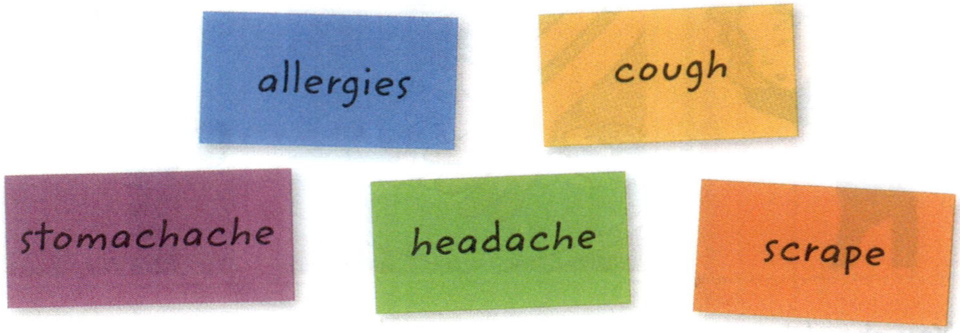

Choose a card. Tell your partner about your problem.

Your partner will give you advice.

Continue with the rest of the cards.

Vocabulary and Grammar | Review

24 Complete the dialogues with *should* or *shouldn't*.

1. **A:** Oh, no. I cut myself.
   B: You ________________ clean the cut and put a bandage on it.
2. **A:** I'm so sleepy today.
   B: You ________________ stay up so late at night.
3. **A:** I have a stomachache.
   B: You ________________ eat so many sweets.
4. **A:** My allergies are really bad today.
   B: You ________________ take some medicine and stay in the house.

cough	fever
scrape	sore throat
stomachache	toothache

25 Write the name of the ailment each person has.

1. stomachache 2. ________________ 3. ________________

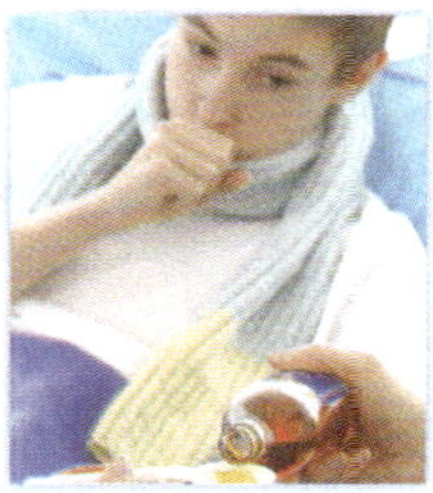

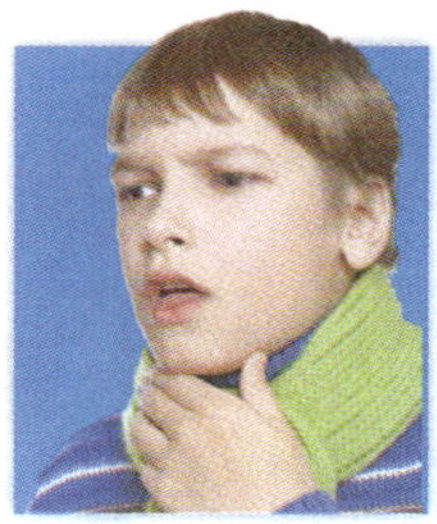

4. ________________ 5. ________________ 6. ________________

26 Answer the questions. Write sentences.

1. What should you do to stay healthy?

____

2. What shouldn't you do to stay healthy?

____

I Can
- [ ] **talk about illnesses and ailments.**
- [ ] **give advice.**

unit 5 Weird and Wild ANIMALS

A43 1 **Listen and read. Then sing.**

Understanding Animals

Do you know a lot about animals and
All the different types there are?
Some are big, and some are small,
And some are just bizarre!

Understanding animals is good for us to do.
Learning about animals helps us and helps them, too!

Some live in trees or in the sea,
And some live where it's hot.
Some are beautiful, and some are cute,
And some are . . . well, they're not!

(Chorus)

It's important to learn about animals,
Though many seem strange, it's true.
When we learn about animals,
We learn about ourselves, too.

(Chorus)

A44

2 Listen and say the names of the animals.

1. whistling spider

- Live in ______________
- About ______ centimeters (cm) wide

2. glass frog

- Live in Central and South ______________
- ______ meters (m) long

3. angler fish

- Live in ______________ all over the world
- Female: ______ cm long
- Male: ______ cm long

4. Angora rabbit

- Many live in ______________
- Weighs about ______ kilograms (kg)

5. coconut crab

- Live on many islands in the ______________ Ocean
- About ______ cm wide

6. tarsier

- Live in Southeast ______________
- Body: ______ cm long
- Tail: ______ cm long

A45

3 Listen. Fill in the information in 2. Use the words and numbers from the box.

America	Asia	Australia	Europe	Pacific	oceans
0.5 3	4	5 10	20	22	25

4 THINK BIG Answer the questions with a partner.

1. Which animals do you think are weird? Why?
2. What else would you like to learn about these animals?
3. Do you know about other weird animals? Explain.

A46–47 **5** **Listen and read.**

5 Scientists are studying chimpanzees to find out more about how they live.

6 Adam wonders whether chimps are nicer than some people.

READING COMPREHENSION

sign language smart talk tools

6 Read and complete.

1. Chimps are very ________________ animals.
2. Chimps ________________ to each other.
3. Some chimps learn to use ________________ to talk to people.
4. Chimps sometimes use ________________ to get their food.

7 THINK BIG Ask and answer with a partner.

1. What makes chimpanzees such amazing animals?
2. What else do you know about chimpanzees?
3. There aren't many chimpanzees left in the world today. Why do you think this is?

Language in Action

A48
8 **Listen and read. Say.**

Jane: Wow, listen to this. Tigers are endangered. There are only 3,200 of them left in the world today.

Ted: Really?

Jane: Yes. In the 1900s, there were more than 100,000 tigers.

Ted: Wow! Why are there only 3,200 now?

Jane: Because some people kill tigers. They sell them for their fur or to make medicine.

Ted: That's terrible!

Jane: I know. But some people are trying to help them.

Ted: Maybe we can help them, too.

Jane: We can. Learning about tigers is the best way to start.

9 **Practice the dialogue in 8 with a partner.**

A49
10 **Listen and stick. Label each picture with the animal's name.**

bumblebee bat | Egyptian tortoise | Mexican walking fish | red panda

1. ______________ 2. ______________ 3. ______________ 4. ______________

A49
11 **THINK BIG** **Listen again. Why is each of the animals endangered? Write your ideas in your notebook and share them with the class.**

How many chimpanzees were there 100 years ago?	There **were** more than one million. But now there **are** only about 200,000.

12 **Complete the sentences with *how many*, *there were*, and *there are*.**

1. How many Komodo dragons were there fifty years ago? There were more than 20,000. But now there are probably fewer than 5,000 in the Komodo Islands.
2. __________ Andean condors were there in the past? __________ many Andean condors in the mountains of South America. But now __________ only a few thousand left.
3. __________ volcano rabbits were there fifty years ago? __________ only about 1,000. We don't know how many __________ now, but probably only a few hundred.
4. __________ Tasmanian devils were there twenty-five years ago? __________ more than 100,000 Tasmanian devils. But now __________ only about 20,000.

Why are chimpanzees endangered?	They're endangered **because** people are moving into their habitat.

13 **Read and talk about why these animals are endangered.**

1. Why are Komodo dragons endangered?
   People are killing them. / People are moving into their habitat.
2. Why are Andean condors endangered?
   Other animals are killing them. / They are getting sick and dying.
3. Why are volcano rabbits endangered?
   People are destroying their habitat. / There is too much pollution.
4. Why are Tasmanian devils endangered?
   People are killing them. / People are moving into their habitat.

14 **Work with a partner and find out more about each of the animals in 12 and 13. Discuss.**

CONTENT WORDS

breed domestic evolved naturally purposely wolf

A50

15 **Listen and read.**

People's Best Friend

The domestic dog is one of the world's most popular pets. There are over 150 breeds, or types, of dogs. Most scientists agree that dogs evolved from wolves—about 15,000 years ago.

Many of the dog breeds we know today evolved over the years. Some became shorter and heavier. Some developed longer or shorter fur. Many of these changes happened naturally. However, many breeds came about because people purposely bred them to do different jobs.

Poodles Because poodles often have fancy haircuts, many people think of them as the "super models" of the dog world. However, poodles are really working dogs. They are strong and smart, and they are good swimmers and hunters. Poodles often work as guard dogs, too.

Jack Russell Terriers Jack Russell terriers are small dogs. However, they are one of the hardest working breeds. Many Jack Russell terriers today are pets. But a hundred years ago, these dogs had an important job: to keep rats and mice off farms.

Italian Greyhounds The Italian greyhound is an old dog breed. These dogs were popular with kings and queens in Europe over 500 years ago. Do you know why? With no electricity, the castles of Europe were very cold. People used Italian greyhounds to warm their beds before they went to sleep!

16 **Read and match.**

1. The Italian greyhound is ____ a. dogs evolved from wolves.
2. Jack Russell terriers ____ b. kept mice and rats away.
3. Poodles are ____ c. an old dog breed.
4. Scientists agree that ____ d. good swimmers.

A51

17 **Listen and read.**

Dragons

Dragons are mythical creatures. That means they are not real. They are important mythical animals in many cultures around the world. North America, South America, Europe, Africa, Oceania, and Asia all have stories about dragons in their history. Antarctica is the only continent in the world with no connection to dragons! But different cultures see dragons differently.

In Asia In Japan, China, and Korea, dragons are beautiful and magical creatures. Some stories about them are more than 4,000 years old. Asian dragons do not have wings. They look like giant lizards. In Asia, dragons are not scary. They are good. They help people.

In the West In Europe, North America, and South America, stories about dragons usually show them as evil. Western dragons have giant wings, and they breathe fire. Western dragons are usually scary. However, there are some stories of good dragons in Western culture.

In Australia and Oceania Dragons have a very long history in Australia and Oceania, too. Some stories of dragons in Oceania are more than 50,000 years old. These dragons are called *bunyip*. In stories, the bunyip is a scary monster made of different parts of many animals.

The only real dragon alive today is the Komodo dragon, a very large lizard that lives on a small island in Indonesia. The Komodo dragon is now an endangered species. Many people are trying to help save the world's only living dragon from extinction.

18 **THINK BIG** **Discuss the questions with a classmate.**

1. What stories do you know about dragons? Explain.
2. Which of the dragons on this page do you like best? Why?
3. What do you know about the Komodo dragon?

Writing | End Marks

A sentence may end with a period (.), a question mark (?), or an exclamation point (!). These are called end marks.

Use a period at the end of a sentence that makes a statement.

I like stories about dragons.

Use a question mark at the end of a direct question.

Do you have a pet?

If you want a statement to show strong feeling, use an exclamation point at the end.

The whistling spider is scary!

19 **Rewrite each sentence with a period, a question mark, or an exclamation point.**

1. There are many organizations that help endangered animals
2. Look at those fantastic dragons
3. Can glass frogs swim
4. Where do Komodo dragons live
5. Angora rabbits are so soft
6. I like to play with my cat

20 **Write your own sentences. Write one with a period, one with a question mark, and one with an exclamation point.**

A52

21 Listen and write the number. Write the sentence under the correct picture.

Don't pollute animal habitats. Make space for wildlife. Reduce, reuse, recycle.

____ ____ ____

______________________ ______________________ ______________________

______________________ ______________________ ______________________

22 Discuss what you can do to help take care of animals and their habitats.

What can we do to protect endangered species?

We can protect their habitats.

PROJECT

23 Make Conservation signs. Post your signs in the halls of your school.

24 **Read about these endangered animals.**

Name: Asian elephant

100 years ago: 90,000

Now: 45,000

Why endangered: People are killing them.

Name: Black rhinoceros

100 years ago: 300,000

Now: 2,000

Why endangered: People are killing them.

Name: Cheetah

100 years ago: more than 100,000

Now: 12,000

Why endangered: Their habitat is disappearing.

Name: Polar bear

100 years ago: No one knows

Now: 20,000

Why endangered: The climate is changing.

Name: Andean flamingo

100 years ago: No one knows

Now: 34,000

Why endangered: Their habitat's polluted.

Name: Tiger

100 years ago: 100,000

Now: 3,200

Why endangered: People are killing them.

25 **Work in pairs. Ask and answer questions about the endangered animals on this page.**

How many cheetahs were there 100 years ago?

How many are there now?

Why are they endangered?

There were more than 100,000.

There are only 12,000.

Their habitat is disappearing.

26 **Complete the sentences with *there are* or *there were*.**

1. Yesterday, ________________ three kids at the animal rescue meeting. Today, ________________ eight kids at the meeting.
2. ________________ five horses on the farm last year. Now, ________________ six.
3. ________________ twelve boys on the team last week, but ________________ only ten this week.
4. ________________ lots of cookies in this jar before lunch. Now ________________ none left!

27 **Label the pictures.**

chimpanzee | coconut crab | tarsier

1. ________________ 2. ________________ 3. ________________

28 **Find out more. Research answers to the questions below.**

1. Are there any endangered animals in the area where you live? Explain.

____

2. Why are they endangered?

____

3. What can you do to help them?

____

I Can

☐ **talk about different kinds of animals.**

☐ **tell why certain animals are endangered.**

unit 6

Life Long AGO

B1 1 **Listen and read. Then sing.**

In the Old Days

Life one hundred years ago
Was different, you see.
There were no computers,
And there was no TV.

Life was different in the old days.
Life was different in so many ways.

People got their water
From pumps or wells outdoors.
Now we just turn on the tap,
And out fresh water pours!

(Chorus)

Life was so much slower!
Few people owned a car.
Most kids had to walk to school,
And they walked pretty far!

(Chorus)

B2

2 Listen and say.

NOW

1. drive cars

2. use a washing machine

3. use a cell phone

4. use electric lights

5. use a microwave

6. watch TV

LONG AGO

____ a. used a coal stove

____ b. used a phone with an operator

1 c. traveled by horse and buggy

____ d. washed clothes by hand

____ e. used oil lamps

____ f. listened to the radio

B3

3 Match the activities we do today with activities people did long ago in 2. Write the number. Then listen and check.

4 THINK BIG What else is different now? Tell a partner.

5 Listen and read.

Life Was Nicer Then

1 Billy is watching TV and doesn't want to get off the sofa.

2 Billy's grandmother doesn't want Billy to be lazy.

3 Most TVs didn't have remote controls when Billy's grandmother was a kid.

4 Billy's grandmother thinks life was a lot nicer when she was young.

5 But now Billy's grandmother uses a microwave to make dinner.

6 Maybe some things about modern life are nicer!

READING COMPREHENSION

6 **Look at the story. Circle the correct word or words to complete the sentences.**

When Billy's grandmother was a kid . . .

1. People **watched / didn't watch** TV.
2. People **had / didn't have** remote controls to change channels.
3. Life **was / wasn't** simpler and quieter.
4. People **cooked / didn't cook** food in a microwave.

7 THINK BIG **Ask and answer with a partner.**

1. Why doesn't Billy's grandmother give him the remote control?
2. What kinds of remote controls do you have in your home?
3. Why do you think Billy's grandmother uses a microwave oven to cook food?

Language in Action

B6

8 **Listen and read. Say.**

Millie: Who's that?

Mom: That's a picture of your great-great-grandparents.

Millie: But they're so young!

Mom: Oh, well, this picture is from 1905. That was a long time ago.

Millie: How did people go places in 1905?

Mom: They used to ride a horse and buggy, or they walked.

Millie: Did you use to ride a horse and buggy, Mom?

Mom: I'm not *that* old!

9 **Practice the dialogue in 8 with a partner.**

B7

10 **Listen and stick. Write the number.**

 ____

 ____

 ____

 ____

B7

11 **THINK BIG** **Listen again. What do you think life was like before we had the modern inventions from 10? Write your ideas in your notebook and share with the class.**

Did people **have** cars in 1950?	Yes, they **did**.
Did people **have** cars in 1900?	No, they **didn't**. They traveled by horse and buggy or by train.

12 **Read the questions. Complete the answers.**

1. Did your father have a car in high school?

   No, he didn't. He used to ride a bicycle.

2. Did people have video games twenty years ago?

   ____________ There were some very popular video games back then.

3. Did your grandmother have a computer?

   ____________ She never used a computer.

4. Did people have running water in their homes 200 years ago?

   ____________ They used to get water from a pump outside.

5. Did people write letters in the past?

   ____________ Now we write letters and send emails.

Before TV, what **did** people **use to do** for entertainment at night?	They **used to listen** to the radio.

13 **Read the questions and answer them with your own ideas. Use *used to* in your answers.**

1. Before computers, what did people use to do to keep in touch?

   ____

2. Before cell phones, what did people use to do to call each other?

   ____

3. Before microwave, what did people use to do to cook their food?

   ____

14 **Work with a partner. Ask and answer questions like the ones in 13. Look at pages 66–67 for ideas.**

CONTENT WORDS

average speed | distance traveled | equation | number of hours

B8

15 **Listen and read. Complete the equations to solve the word problems.**

Multiplication

1. **Horse and Buggy** Until the early 1900s, many people traveled by horse and buggy. A horse and buggy had an average speed of 5 miles (8 km) per hour. If a horse and buggy travels for 4 hours, how far does it travel?

_____ x _____ = _____

average speed | number of hours | distance traveled

2. **Model T** In 1908, the Model T Ford became one of the first popular cars in the world. The average speed of a Model T was about 25 miles (40 km) per hour. If a Model T travels for 4 hours, how far does it travel?

_____ x _____ = _____

average speed | number of hours | distance traveled

3. **Modern Car** Cars today are much faster than they were in the past. The average speed of a modern car is about 56 miles (90 km) per hour. If a person travels in a modern car for 4 hours, about how far does he or she travel?

_____ x _____ = _____

average speed | number of hours | distance traveled

16 **Make up your own equations. Read them to a partner. Ask your partner to complete them.**

17 Listen and read.

Low-Tech Tribes

Could you live without a computer or a cell phone? It might be hard for you to imagine a life without technology. But many people live happily without it.

The Maasai

The Maasai people of Kenya, in Africa, are one of the most famous tribes on the planet. The Maasai are *nomadic*. This means they do not live in one place all the time. They move from place to place and make new homes each time they move. They build their homes in the forests from things they can find in nature—mud, sticks, grass, and rocks. Their villages do not have running water or electricity.

The Hmong

The Hmong people of Southeast Asia live in parts of Thailand, Laos, and Vietnam. They have their own language and their own way of life. They live the same way now that their ancestors lived 2,000 years ago. You won't find much technology in a Hmong village.

The Koryak

The Koryak people live in Russia, on the northern part of the Pacific Coast. The land is Arctic tundra, which is very cold. For food, these people catch fish or herd reindeer. This picture shows Koryak children cooking food for their family. They are wearing warm hats made of reindeer skins.

18 THINK BIG Discuss these questions with a classmate.

1. Do you know of any other tribes or groups of people who live without using technology?
2. Do you think you could live without technology? Why or why not?

Writing | Quotation Marks

Quotation marks (" ") come in pairs. You put quotation marks around the words that people say.

> "I had a great time at my grandpa's house," said Jaime.
> "Did they watch TV back then?" he asked.
> Miguel said, "I got a new cell phone for my birthday!"

Commas, periods, question marks, and exclamation points usually go inside quotation marks.

19 **Put quotation marks in the correct places in the sentences.**

1. I just saw a movie about Henry Ford and the Model T, he said.
2. What should we do this weekend? she asked.
3. Do your homework before watching TV! his mother told him.
4. Taylor said, I really want a new computer for my birthday.
5. You need to finish your book report by Friday, said Mr. Clark.
6. Happy birthday, Grandma Rose! everyone yelled.

20 **Write your own sentences using quotation marks.**

1. ______________________________
2. ______________________________
3. ______________________________
4. ______________________________
5. ______________________________

B1 21

21 Read and listen. Number the steps in order.

Solving a Problem!

☐ Gather Information

☐ Review and Learn

☐ Use the Best Idea

☐ Develop Ideas

☐ Define the Problem

22 Talk about what you can do to solve problems in your classroom.

Our class needs a new computer.

I agree. How can we raise enough money to buy one?

PROJECT

23 Make a **Problem-Solving** worksheet. Work as a group and use the worksheet to solve this problem.

Steps	Details
1. Define the problem.	Our class needs to raise money for a new computer.
2. Gather information.	
3. Develop ideas.	
4. Use the best idea.	
5. Review and learn.	

Review | Listening and Speaking

24 THINK BIG **Work with a partner. Find the differences between the two pictures. Make a list. Tell a partner.**

A long time ago, people used to wash their clothes by hand.

Now many people use washing machines to wash clothes.

LONG AGO

NOW

Compare lists with other students in your class. Make a class list.

25 Complete the dialogue.

did didn't have to use used

A: Life in the old days was hard. They didn't __________ to have electricity, you know.

B: Really? No electric lights? What __________ they use to light their homes?

A: People __________ to use candles and oil lamps for light.

B: Wow. Did they __________ washing machines back then?

A: No, they __________. People used to wash their clothes by hand. And they didn't have TVs.

B: No TVs?

A: That's right. People used __________ listen to the radio for entertainment.

26 Complete the sentences about each photo.

cook	use
drive	watch
make	write

1. It is easy to __________ emails.

2. It is easy to __________ a washing machine.

3. It's fun to __________ TV with my family.

4. I __________ calls on my cell phone.

5. Microwaves __________ food quickly.

6. My mother likes to __________ her car.

I Can

- [ ] **talk about the past and the present.**
- [ ] **talk about what people used to do.**

How Well Do I Know It? Can I Use It?

1 Read and circle.

I know this. I need more practice. I don't know this.

	PAGES			
Ailments: allergies, coughing, scrape, stomachache . . .	42–43			
Remedies: drink some juice, get some rest, take some aspirin, see a dentist . . .	42, 46–47			
Endangered animals: angler fish, chimpanzees, komodo dragons, red pandas, tigers . . .	55, 57–59			
Activities (present): drive cars, use electric lights, use a microwave, watch TV . . . **Activities (past):** listened to the radio, washed clothes by hand, traveled by horse and buggy . . .	66–67			
You **should** take some aspirin. She **shouldn't** stay up late. They should take care of **themselves.**	47			
How many chimpanzees were there 100 years ago? There **were** more than 1,000,000. But now there **are** only about 200,000.	58–59			
Did people **have** coal stoves 100 years ago? Yes, they **did**. **Did** people **have** computers 100 years ago? No, they **didn't**.	70–71			
Before TV, what **did** people **use to do** for entertainment? They **used to read** or **listen** to the radio.	70–71			

I Can Do It!

B11

2 **Get ready.**

didn't use to watch
should go outside
should watch
shouldn't watch
used to go outside

A. Complete the dialogue. Use the words from the box. Then listen and check.

Mom: What's the matter, Kevin?

Kevin: My eyes hurt.

Mom: I know why. You watch too much TV! And look at Spike.

Kevin: Why? What's the matter with him?

Mom: He's out of shape. Both of you _______________ and get some exercise.

Kevin: Oh, Mom!

Mom: Listen, I think you _______________ so much TV. You spend too much time looking at monitors—TV, computer, and cell phone.

Kevin: So . . . ?

Mom: That's why your eyes hurt. You _______________ TV for no more than one hour a day.

Kevin: Only one hour?

Mom: Yes. A long time ago, people _______________ TV all the time.

Kevin: What did they do?

Mom: Well, they _______________ and play. So go! And take Spike.

Kevin: Oh, OK, Mom. Come on, Spike.

B. Practice the dialogue in **A** with a partner.

C. Ask and answer the questions with a partner.

1. What do you think of Kevin's mom's advice?
2. Do you think you should watch less TV? Why or why not?
3. What do both people and pets need to stay healthy?

3 Get set.

STEP 1 Cut out the cards on page 125.

STEP 2 Arrange the cards face down in two stacks: green cards and orange cards. Now you're ready to **Go!**

4 Go!

A. Read the dialogues.

Dialogue A	Dialogue B
A: What's the matter?	**A:** What's the matter?
B: I have a stomachache.	**B:** I have a stomachache.
A: Why?	**A:** Why?
B: I watched too much TV.	**B:** I ate too many French fries.
A: That doesn't make sense.	**A:** You should go see the school nurse.

B. Now play the game. Pick one green card and one orange card. Use them to make up a dialogue like the ones above with a partner. Does the dialogue make sense? If not, pick another orange card. Keep picking orange cards until your dialogue makes sense. When your dialogue makes sense, give advice to your partner. Then switch roles and play the game again.

You should go see the school nurse.

C. Act out one of the dialogues for your class.

5 **Write about yourself.**

- Do you live a healthy lifestyle? Explain.
- Do you think people today have a healthier lifestyle than people 100 years ago? Why or why not?
- What endangered animals do you know about?
- Why are these animals endangered?
- What can people do to help them?

All About Me

Date: ____________

____

____

____

____

How Well Do I Know It Now?

6 **Read and circle.**

A. **Go to page 78. Read and circle again. Use a different color.**

B. **Check (✔).**

- ☐ I can start the next unit.
- ☐ I can ask my teacher for help and then start the next unit.
- ☐ I can practice and then start the next unit.

7 **Rate this Checkpoint. Check the boxes.**

☐	☐	☐	☐	☐	☐	☐
very easy	easy	hard	very hard	fun	OK	not fun

1 2 3 4 5 6 7 8 9

unit 7 Special DAYS

B12 **1 Listen and read. Then sing.**

Special Days Are Fun!

This Friday is a special day—
The last day of the year.
We're going to stay up very late.
At midnight we're going to cheer!

Special days are cool. Special days are fun.
Special days bring special treats for everyone!

Every January first,
We celebrate and say,
"Happy New Year!" to everyone
Because it's New Year's Day.

(Chorus)

There are lots of special days,
And each one is a treat.
We have parades and fireworks
And delicious food to eat.

B13

2 Listen and say.

my birthday

my parents' anniversary

New Year's Eve / Day

Valentine's Day

Independence Day

Earth Day

B14

3 Listen. Then tell a partner how you celebrate special days with your family.

give / get a card

give / get presents

have a party

watch a parade

watch fireworks

eat special foods

4 THINK BIG Answer the questions with a partner.

1. What other special days can you name?
2. What are your favorite special days? Why?
3. What other things do you do on special days?

Story

B15–16 **5** **Listen and read.**

1 Gwen's parents' wedding anniversary is on the tenth.

2 Gwen wants to help her parents celebrate their anniversary.

3 She and her parents are going to go out for a special dinner.

4 Gwen planned a little party after the dinner.

5 Gwen's parents like the plans, but there's a little problem.

6 Gwen got the day right, but the month wrong!

READING COMPREHENSION

6 **Circle *T* for *true* and *F* for *false*.**

	True	False
1. In the story, the next day is June tenth.	T	F
2. Gwen is making a cake for her parents.	T	F
3. Gwen is right about the day but wrong about the month.	T	F
4. Gwen's parents' anniversary is on June tenth.	T	F

7 THINK BIG **Ask and answer these questions with a partner.**

1. How do you think Gwen feels at the end of the story?
2. What do you think Gwen's parents are going to say next?
3. What is your favorite thing about celebrating special days such as birthdays or anniversaries?

B17

8 **Listen and read. Say.**

Calvin: When are we going to go to Grandma and Grandpa's house?

Mom: On the thirteenth.

Calvin: This Saturday? Are we going to have a big party for Grandma's birthday?

Mom: Yes, on Sunday. I can't believe it. She's going to be 70 years old! Don't forget to get a card for her.

Calvin: Don't worry. I'm making one for her now.

9 **Practice the dialogue in 8 with a partner.**

B18

10 **Listen and stick. Label the pictures with the name of the special day.**

anniversary
Earth Day
New Year's Eve
Valentine's Day

1. ____________________

2. ____________________

3. ____________________

4. ____________________

11 THINK BIG **Work with a partner. Act out some of the things you do on special days. Ask your partner to guess.**

When **are**	you	**going to have** the party?	I	**am going to have** it on Monday.
	they		We	**are going to have** it on Monday.
			They	
When **is**	he / she	**going to visit** Grandma?	He / She	**is going to visit** her next month.

12 **Write the responses using the words in parentheses.**

1. When are we going to have our test? *(Monday)*

____

2. When is she going to visit her cousins? *(next week)*

____

3. When are they going to have a concert? *(this Friday)*

____

Are you/they going to visit Grandma **on the ninth**?	Yes, **on the ninth**.
Is he/she going to visit Grandma **on the fifth**?	No, **on the ninth**.

B19

13 **Listen and read. Say the ordinal numbers.**

1st first	2nd second	3rd third	4th fourth		
5th fifth	6th sixth	7th seventh	8th eighth	9th ninth	10th tenth
11th eleventh	12th twelfth	13th thirteenth	14th fourteenth	15th fifteenth	16th sixteenth
17th seventeenth	18th eighteenth	19th nineteenth	20th twentieth	21st twenty-first	30th thirtieth

14 **Complete the sentences with true answers.**

1. Today is the ______________________.
2. Tomorrow is the ______________________.
3. Yesterday was the ______________________.
4. Next Monday is the ______________________.

15 **Work with a partner and talk about people you are going to visit.**

CONTENT WORDS

calendar celebrate divided extra leap million

B20

16 **Listen and read.**

Leap Year

How Long Is a Year? Most people say a year is 365 days. It takes about 365 days for Earth to travel around the sun. However, it actually takes a little longer for Earth to go around the sun. In fact, it takes 365 days, 5 hours, 49 minutes, and 12 seconds.

If a calendar has only 365 days, what happens to the extra 5 hours, 49 minutes, and 12 seconds? The answer is this: Every four years, we add a day to the calendar. It's February 29, and it's called *leap day*. This kind of year is called a *leap year*. A leap year has 366 days.

Leap-Day Babies People who are born on February 29 are called *leap-day babies*, or *leapers*. There are about four million leapers in the world. When do they celebrate their birthday? Do they celebrate only once every four years? Some leapers celebrate it on February 28, and others celebrate it on March 1. Think about it: A twelve-year-old leaper may have celebrated only three birthdays on the actual day he or she was born!

Which Years Are Leap Years? Years that can be divided evenly by four are leap years. The year 2000 was a leap year. Then 2004, 2008, and 2012 were the next leap years. If you know a leaper, make sure you say, "Happy birthday!" Your chance to do that comes only once every four years!

17 **Circle the leap years.**

1996 1994

2002 2012

2018

2020

B21

18 **Listen and read.**

Unusual Festivals

The world is full of strange and interesting festivals. Here are just a few of the most unusual festivals in the world.

Holi—The Festival of Colors

This festival takes place every year in India, Nepal, and many other parts of the world in the spring. Holi lasts for many days. During Holi, people throw colored powder and water at each other. Holi is a festival to celebrate the end of winter and the arrival of spring. It is one of the most colorful festivals in the world.

Tomatina—The Tomato Festival

Every year, on the last Wednesday of August, there is an interesting festival in Buñol, Spain. People come from all over the world for a big food fight. Tomatina is the festival of throwing tomatoes! All over the city, people run through the streets throwing red tomatoes at each other. It is a really messy festival, but everyone has a good time.

The Monkey Buffet

On the last weekend in November, the people of Lopburi, Thailand, invite some unusual guests to dinner. Hundreds of monkeys live near the town. Once every year, the monkeys are invited to a feast. The monkeys feast on fruit, nuts, and vegetables. People from all over the world come to watch the monkeys eat.

Qoyllurit'i—Festival of the Snows

One of the strangest and coldest festivals on Earth takes place every May on a glacier in Peru. Each year about 30,000 people go to the festival known as Qoyllurit'i. For three days and nights people celebrate with music and dancing on top of the glacier. At the end of the festival, everyone walks out together carrying torches of fire.

19 **THINK BIG** **Discuss these questions with a classmate.**

1. Which of these festivals would you like to see? Why?
2. Do you know of any other unusual festivals? Explain.

20 Take a look at the parts of an email:

FROM elena@bigenglish.com ← The email address of the sender

TO diego@bigenglish.com ← The email address of the receiver

SUBJECT Our new computer ← What your email is about

Dear Diego, ← The *greeting* starts the message.

Guess what! We got a new computer in my house. I'm so happy! Now I can play computer games at home. I can use the computer for homework, too.

This is my first email on the new computer. Send me a message soon! I'm going to write some more emails now.

← The *body* is the main part of the message.

Your friend,
Elena
← The *closing* and the *signature* end the message.

21 Write a reply to the email in **20**.

FROM

TO

SUBJECT

22 Write a definition for the word *tradition*.

23 Look and listen. Number the traditions in order. B22

24 Talk about some of your family traditions.

Does your family have a special tradition for New Year's Eve?

Yes. We always eat noodles on New Year's Eve!

PROJECT

25 Make a **Traditions Around the World** poster. Display your posters in the hallways of your school.

26 **Play the *Holiday Plans* game.**

Sit in a circle. Choose one holiday with the class.
Student A says what he/she is going to do.

Student B talks about Student A, and then adds one activity.

Continue around the group. Each student has to use a different activity.

Try to continue with the whole class!

27 **Complete the dialogue.**

am	on	on
are	are	are
to	going	

Mom: It's your dad's birthday this month.
Mike: Is it ______________ the twenty-seventh?
Mom: No, it's ______________ the twenty-second.
Mike: What ______________ we going to do for him?
Mom: We're ______________ to have a little party.
Mike: ______________ we going to go out?
Mom: No, we're going ______________ have the party at home. Aunt Heather and Uncle Troy ______________ going to come over, and I ______________ going to make a special dinner for all of us.
Mike: That sounds like fun.

28 **Label the pictures.**

Earth Day
Independence Day
New Year's Eve
Valentine's Day

1. ______________

2. ______________

3. ______________

4. ______________

29 **Find out more. Research and answer the questions about one of the holidays in 28.**

1. When do people celebrate this day?
____
2. What do people do on this day?
____

I Can
- [ ] talk about different kinds of special days and traditions.
- [ ] talk about dates.

unit 8 HOBBIES

B23 1 **Listen and read. Then sing.**

The Best and the Worst

Matthew collects toy cars—
He has one hundred and seven.
But Pam's collection is bigger;
She has three hundred and eleven!

May is good at playing games;
She's really good at chess.
But Paul is even better than May.
And Liz, well, she's the best!

What's your hobby, Bobby?
What do you like to do?
What's your hobby, Bobby?
What is fun for you?

Steve is a terrible singer.
Emma's worse than Steve.
But David's singing is the worst.
When he sings, people leave!

It's good to have a hobby.
Some people have a few.
Even if you're not the best,
It still is fun to do!

(Chorus)

B24

2 Listen and say.

1. coin collection

2. doll collection

3. shell collection

4. toy car collection

5. basketball player

6. chess player

7. soccer player

8. video game player

9. dancer

10. painter

11. singer

12. writer

B25

3 Listen. Write the numbers from 2 under each name. Then tell a partner about each kid.

1. Freddie

4 ____ ____

2. Sylvia

____ ____ ____

3. Philip

____ ____ ____

4. Kayla

____ ____ ____

THINK BIG Answer the questions with a partner.

1. Do you have a collection? What kind?
2. What sports or activities do you like?
3. Which kid in 3 is the most like you? Why?

Freddie has a big toy car collection.

B26–27

5 Listen and read.

The School Play

1 Megan's dad is excited about this year's school play.

2 He wants Megan to be a star!

3 Snow White is the most important character in the play.

4 The Evil Queen is another important character in the play.

5 There aren't many other female characters in the play.

6 Megan's part is very small, but her dad is still proud of her.

READING COMPREHENSION

6 Complete the sentences.

1. Megan is going to be in the ________________ *Snow White*.
2. ________________ is the best singer in the class.
3. ________________ is the best actor in the class.
4. Megan is going to be a ________________ in the school play.

7 THINK BIG Ask and answer these questions with a partner.

1. How does Megan's dad feel about the school play? Why?
2. How does Megan feel about the school play? Why?
3. Do you like performing on stage? Why or why not?

Language in Action

B28

8 **Listen and read. Say.**

Elliot: Paul has a big rock collection.

Matt: Yes, it is big. But Andrea's rock collection is bigger than Paul's.

Elliot: Hmm. Andrea's collection is very big!

Matt: But Taylor has the biggest rock collection of all.

Elliot: Wow! How did Taylor get so many cool rocks?

Matt: His grandfather is a geologist. He studies rocks and sends Taylor new samples every month.

9 **Practice the dialogue in 8 with a partner.**

B29

10 **Listen and stick. Label each picture with a word from the box.**

best	coolest	worst

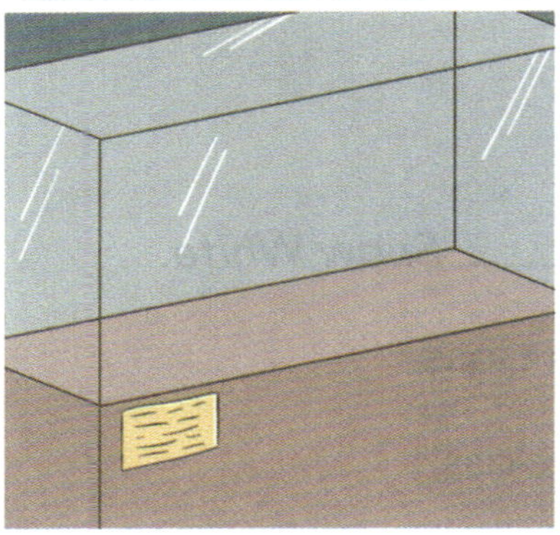

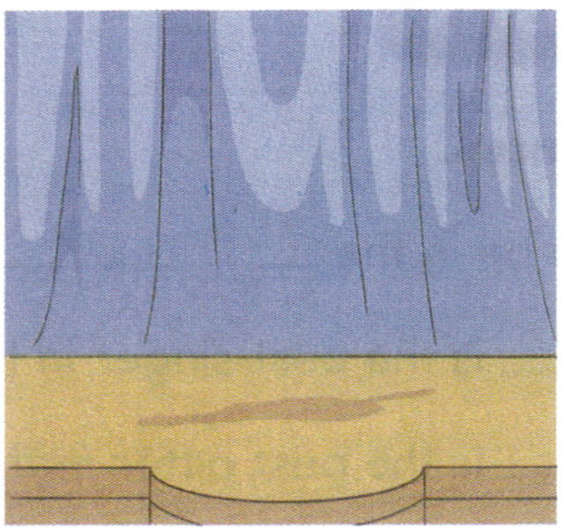

1. ______________ 2. ______________ 3. ______________

11 **THINK BIG Think of people in your family. Talk about the things they can do.**

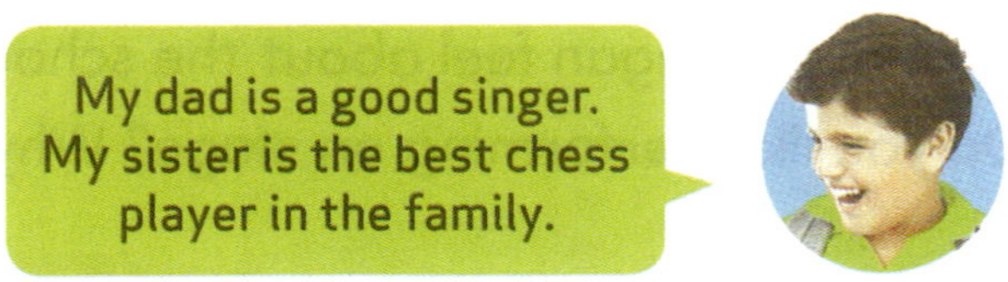

Chris has a **big** stamp collection.
Katie's collection is **bigger** than Chris's collection.
Kyle has **the biggest** stamp collection.

12 **Look at the pictures and complete the dialogues.**

A: Look at that red car. It's really old!

B: Yes. But the blue car is ______________ than the red car.

A: And the black car is the ______________ car of them all.

Laura is a **good** soccer player.	My brother's paintings are **bad**.
Steve is a **better** player **than** Laura.	My sister's paintings are **worse than** his.
Yoko is **the best** soccer player in the class.	My paintings are **the worst** of all.

13 **Look at the pictures. Complete the dialogues.**

1. 

A: Sam is a bad singer.

B: Yes. But Mike is ______________.

A: Yes. But Terry is the ______________ singer of all.

2. 

A: Vincent is a good student.

B: Yes. But Tim is a ______________ one.

A: True! But Louisa is the ______________ student in our class.

14 **Work with a partner and find out more about people in your class. Report your findings to the class.**

CONTENT WORDS

creative future instructions motivate stress successful

B30

15 **Listen and read.**

Hobbies Are Good for You

Scientists say that hobbies can make kids smarter, healthier, and even more successful when they grow up. How?

They Help You Learn When you have a hobby, you learn new things. You have to read instructions. You look at websites, magazines, and books to get more information about your hobby. More reading makes you a better reader and a better learner.

They Help You Be Creative For many hobbies, such as building model cars and making pottery, you have to use your brain as well as your hands. We learn by doing things and by touching things. These kinds of activities make people more creative.

They Motivate You Having a hobby makes you feel good. Scientists say, "When you make something, the 'feel-good' part of your brain gets a message. It makes you feel happy." When we feel happy, we have less stress. Too much stress can make people sick.

They Help You Build Skills People with hobbies learn how to set goals and solve problems. Learning these skills when you are young can help you when you grow up. For some kids, having a hobby can be the first step to finding a satisfying job in the future.

16 **Check (✓) what you learned in the article about having hobbies. Hobbies can help you . . .**

_____ be more creative
_____ have less stress
_____ be more popular
_____ learn better
_____ make other people happy
_____ set goals
_____ solve problems
_____ learn about yourself

B3 17 **Listen and read.**

The World's WEIRDEST Collections

Some museums show us how people used to live a long time ago. But there are other kinds of museums in the world, too. Here are some facts about a few "weird museums."

The Hair Museum A man in Avanos, Turkey, turned a cave into a museum of women's hair. There are more than 16,000 samples of hair at the Hair Museum. Each sample is labeled with the woman's name and the date it was cut. It all started when the man's friend was moving away. She gave him a small sample of her hair to remember her by. When he told the story to others, many of them also gave him samples of their hair.

The Museum of Underwater Art

To visit this museum, you need to swim. In the ocean near Cancún, Mexico, there is a collection of statues. This museum is inside the National Marine Park of the Yucatán Peninsula of Mexico, and it displays more than 400 sculptures. The British artist, Jason deCaires Taylor, wants the animals and plants in the ocean to become part of the artwork.

The International UFO Museum and Research Center

Many people believe that a UFO landed in Roswell, New Mexico, USA, in 1947. If you want to know more about UFOs, you can visit the International UFO Museum and Research Center. The center holds a UFO Festival every year at the museum. At the festival, experts from around the world come to talk about the latest news in UFO research.

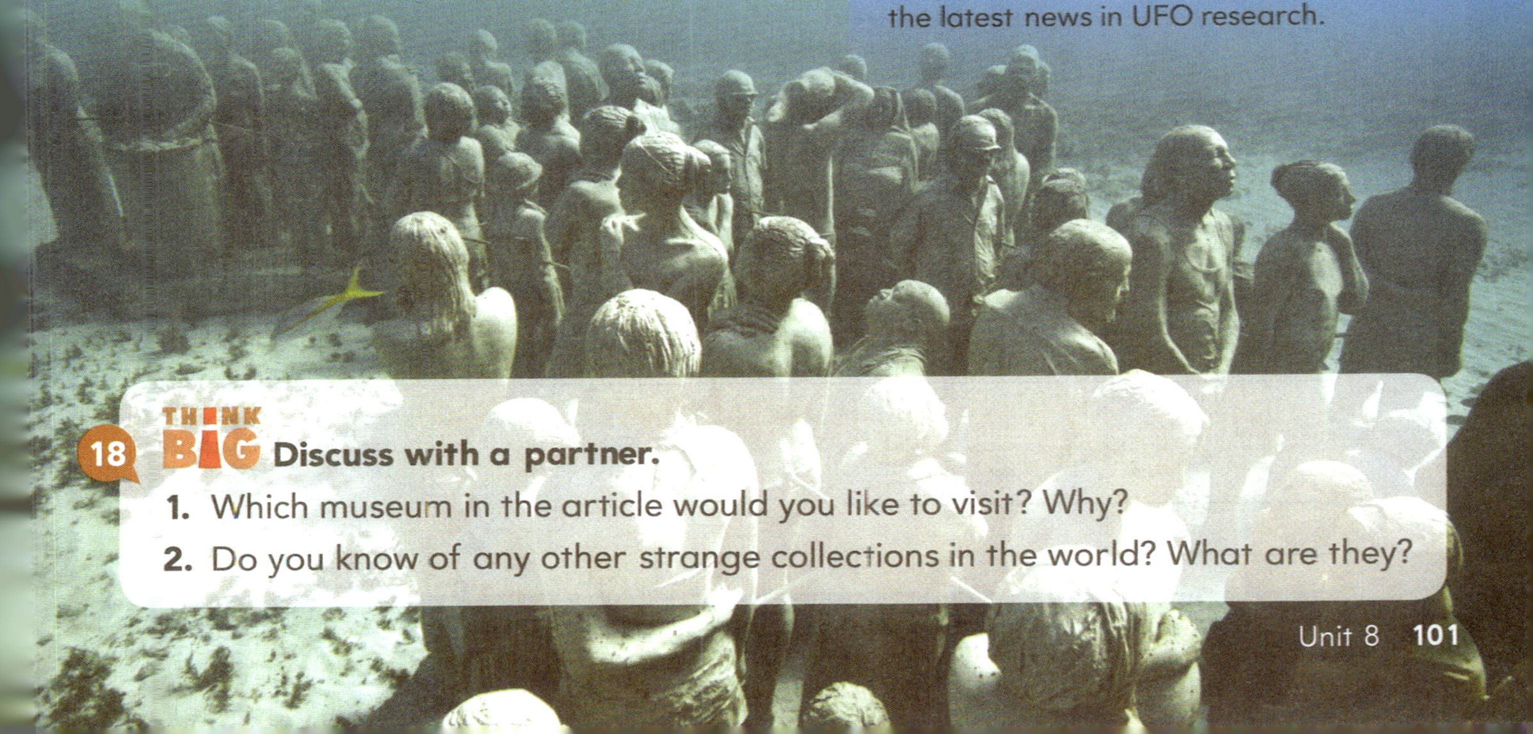

18 THINK BIG **Discuss with a partner.**

1. Which museum in the article would you like to visit? Why?
2. Do you know of any other strange collections in the world? What are they?

Writing | Informal Letters

19 **Take a look at the parts of an informal letter:**

254 N. Summit St.
Smithville, OH 44677 ← Your address

September 15, 2013 ← Today's date

Dear Grandma and Grandpa, ← The *greeting* starts the message.

How are you? I'm fine. School started last week. I'm in the fourth grade now. I'm having a lot of fun in my classes.

I have a new hobby! Uncle Cary taught me how to play chess. It's a little hard, but it's fun, too. I'm learning more about it online. Sometimes I play it with friends from school.

We're going to visit you next month. I can't wait to see you!

← The *body* is the main part of the message.

Love,
Noah ← The *closing* and the *signature* end the message.

20 **Write an informal letter to someone in your family. Tell them about a new hobby. Use the letter in 19 as a model.**

____

____

____

____

____

____

____

____

____

____

____

Be a good sport. | Values in Action

B32

21 Listen and check the kids who are good sports. Write an *X* for the kids who are bad sports.

1. 

_____

2. 

_____

3. 

_____

4. 

_____

22 Role-play with a partner.

You won! It was a good game.

You played well, too.

PROJECT

23 Make a paper bag puppet. Use the puppets to role-play scenes in which they are good sports.

24 **Work in groups of four. Play *Who's the Best?***

Write the numbers *1–4* on small pieces of paper. Put the papers into a small bag.

Each person in the group chooses a number.

Choose one item from the list below. Take turns making sentences about people in your group. Use *better/best* or *worse/worst*. (*1* = *best*, *2* = *better*, *3* = *worse*, and *4* = *worst*)

actor	basketball player	chess player	dancer
painter	singer	soccer player	writer

Choose numbers again and continue with the other items on the list.

25 **Complete the sentences. Use a form of the word in parentheses.**

1. Terrence's shell collection is __________________ than Phoebe's. *(big)*
2. Look at this. This is the __________________ coin in my coin collection. *(old)*
3. The dolls in Sandy's collection are __________________ than my dolls. *(new)*
4. I have a lot of small cars in my collection, but this one is the __________________. *(small)*

26 **Look and complete the sentences.**

1. Mark is a __________________ dancer than Kelly.
2. Sharon is a __________________ dancer than Mark.
3. Sharon is the __________________ dancer in the group.
4. Mark is the __________________ dancer of the three students.

27 **Complete with information about yourself.**

1. I am a good ______________. ______________ is a better ______________ than I am.
2. I am not a good ______________. ______________ is a worse ______________ than I am.

I Can

- [ ] **talk about people's hobbies.**
- [ ] **make comparisons.**

unit 9

Learning New THINGS

B33 1 **Listen and read. Then sing.**

Learning Is Fun

Do you know how to skateboard?
It's so awesome. It's so cool!
I can show you how to do it
On Friday after school.

It's fun to learn new things,
Like how to draw, or bake, or sing!
I wish I had lots more free time.
I would try to learn everything!

I'd like to learn to speak English.
"It's hard!" my friends all say.
But I think it's really interesting.
I'd like to speak it well one day.

(Chorus)

B34

2 Listen and say.

1. dance like a hip-hop artist

2. sing like a rock star

3. bake a cake

4. skateboard

5. play the guitar

6. play tennis

7. speak Chinese

8. draw comic books

9. build a robot

10. make a website

B35

3 Listen. Write the number next to the word you hear.

______ amazing	______ boring	______ cool
______ dangerous	______ difficult	______ interesting

4 THINK BIG Answer the questions with a partner.

1. Which things in 2 can you do? Tell a partner.
2. What do you think about the skills in 2? Use the words from 3 in your answers.
3. Which things in 2 do you want to learn how to do? Why?

Story

5 **Listen and read.**

The Best in the Class

1 Kit and her brother Stan are waiting for the bus. Stan sees a student from Kit's class.

2 Kit thinks Gerald is really smart.

3 Gerald knows how to do a lot of different things.

4 Stan is really impressed.

5 But there are some simple things that Gerald can't do!

6 Gerald is smart about some things but not about everything!

READING COMPREHENSION

6 **Look at the reading. Check the things that Gerald knows how to do.**

_____ **1.** play tennis

_____ **2.** draw comic books

_____ **3.** play the guitar

_____ **4.** make a website

_____ **5.** speak several languages

_____ **6.** bake a cake

7 THINK BIG **Ask and answer with a partner.**

1. What does Kit think of Gerald?
2. Why are Kit and Stan surprised?
3. Do you know how to do any of the things Gerald can do? Which ones would you like to learn to do? Why?

Language in Action

B38

8 **Listen and read. Say.**

James: Do you know how to play the guitar?

Curt: Just a little. Do you know how to play it?

James: No, I don't. But I'd like to learn.

Curt: Me, too. I think it's difficult.

James: Not really. My brother knows how to play. Maybe he can teach us.

Curt: I'd like that!

9 **Practice the dialogue in 8 with a partner.**

B39

10 **Listen and stick. Label the pictures with the phrases from the box.**

learn to dance | learn to draw | learn to play tennis | learn to skateboard

1. ______________________

2. ______________________

3. ______________________

4. ______________________

Do you **know how to play** the piano?			Yes, I do. / No, I don't.	
What would	you	like to learn?	I'd	like to **learn how to play** the piano.
	he/she		He'd/She'd	
	they		They'd	

11 **Complete the questions and answers.**

1. Do you ________________ the guitar?

   ________________. But I can play the piano.

2. Do you ________________ tennis?

   ________________. I play tennis every weekend.

12 **Look at the pictures. Read the questions and write answers.**

1. What would they like to learn?
   They'd like to learn how to build a robot.

2. What would she like to learn?
   ____

3. What would he like to learn?
   ____

What **do**	you	**think of** tennis?	I	**think** it's a lot of fun.
	they		We	
			They	
What **does**	he/she	**think of** ballet?	He/She	**thinks** it's boring.

13 **Ask and answer questions with a partner.**

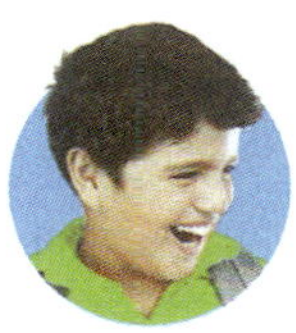

What do you think of hip-hop music?

I think it's amazing.

Connections | Science

CONTENT WORDS

contract joints muscles nerves organs relax

14 **Listen and read.**

Moving Your Body

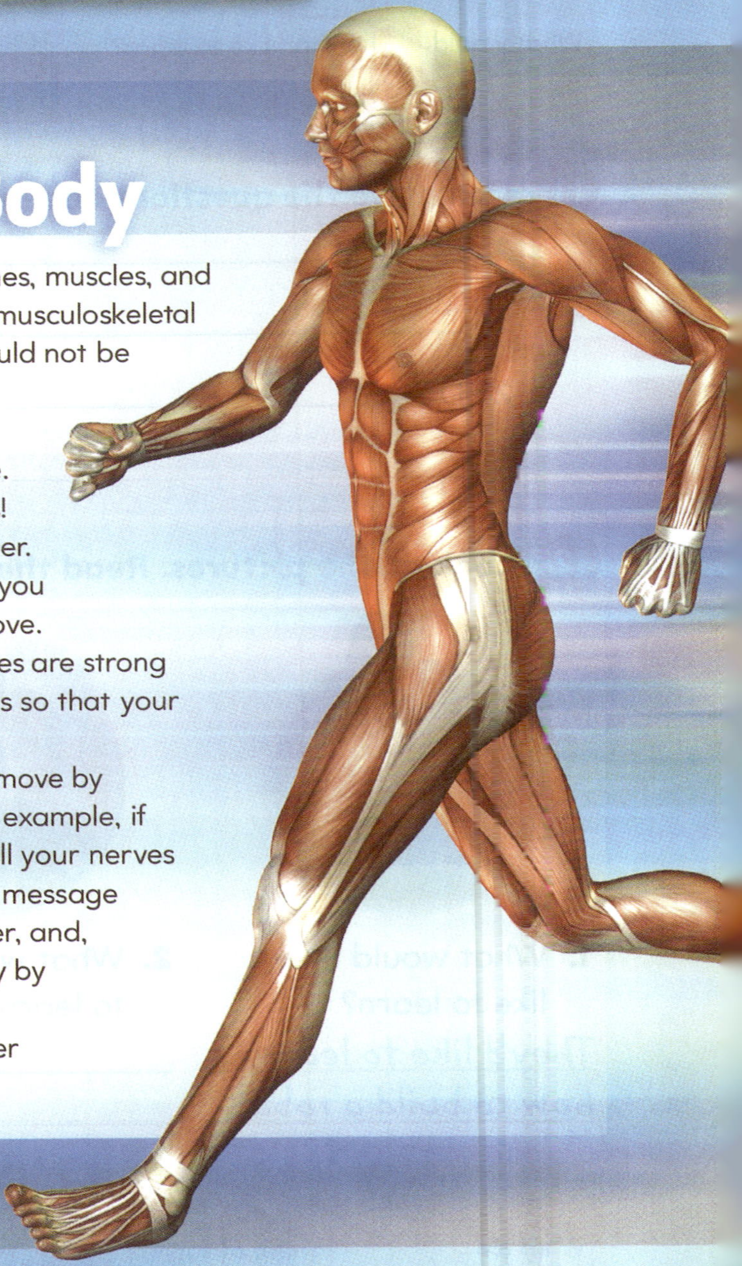

With every move you make, you are using your bones, muscles, and joints. These three kinds of body parts make up your musculoskeletal system. Without your musculoskeletal system, you would not be able to stand, walk, or move in any way.

Your bones are your body's frame. They support the organs within your body and give the body shape. Without bones, your body would look like an octopus!

Your joints connect two or more bones to each other. Joints are important. They allow you to be flexible. If you didn't have joints, your body would not be able to move.

Your muscles are also important for motion. Muscles are strong and flexible. They pull the bones in different directions so that your body moves.

Of course, your muscles, bones, and joints do not move by themselves. Your brain and your nerves help out. For example, if you want to kick a soccer ball, your brain needs to tell your nerves that you want to move your foot. Your nerves send a message to your muscles. Your muscles contract, or get shorter, and, as a result, you kick the ball. Muscles move your body by contracting and then relaxing.

Next time you are rushing to get to class, remember how amazing it is that your body gets you there.

15 **Complete the sentences.**

1. When you want to move, your nerves ____________________ to your muscles.
2. Your bones give your body ____________________.
3. ____________________ are three kinds of body parts that make up your body's musculoskeletal system.
4. Muscles move your body by ____________________.

16 **Listen and read.**

Extraordinary Kids

There are some kids in the world who do things faster and better than most people. Take a look at some of these amazing kids.

Gregory Smith was born in 1990 in Keswick, Virginia, in the United States. Gregory could read before he was two years old. At ten, Gregory started attending college. By sixteen, Gregory had several college degrees. But he is more than just a genius. He travels the world trying to help young people everywhere. He hopes that he can help make the world a safer and more peaceful place for everyone.

At just eight years old, **Yuto Miyazawa** was already a professional musician! He was named "The Youngest Professional Guitarist" by *Guinness Book of World Records* in August, 2008. And he has not stopped since. Yuto has already performed with music legends Ozzy Osbourne, Les Paul, and G. E. Smith. He has appeared on several TV talk shows and performed at Madison Square Garden. Who knows what the future holds for this musical genius?

Many people in Australia are talking about an amazing young artist. **Aelita Andre** started showing her paintings when she was just three. Her father, a famous photographer, says that Aelita started to paint before her second birthday. Many people say that Aelita is too young to be considered a real artist. But her parents are still proud of her work.

Not everyone can be a genius, but everyone has his or her own special talents. What are yours?

17 **THINK BIG** **Discuss with a partner.**

1. Are you surprised by any of the stories in the reading? Which one? Why?
2. Do you know any stories about amazing kids? Describe these kids and what they did.
3. Do you or anyone in your family have any surprising talents? What are they?

Writing | Review

18 **Take a look at the parts of a review.**

Reviewed by **toby23** on March 15 ← Web nickname and date

An Interesting Book for Everyone ← Title of review

★★★★★ ← Rating

Ali and His Camera is an interesting book. ← Topic sentence

I read the book last week and I really liked it. It is not a long book. It has fifteen pages. There are a lot of great pictures in it.

It's about a boy. His name is Ali. He wants a camera. A woman gives him a camera, and he takes pictures. Ali meets a man. The man works at a newspaper. I don't want to tell you too much. You should read it for yourself.

← The body (the main part of the review)

Ali and His Camera is a great book, and I recommend it to everyone! ← Final sentence

19 **Write a review of a book or movie you like. Share your review with the class. Use the review in 18 as a model.**

B42

20 Listen and check the activities that the people want to try. Write an *X* for the things they do not want to try.

1. ______ 2. ______ 3. ______ 4. ______

Role-play with a partner.

Do you know how to build a robot?

No, I don't. But I'd like to learn!

PROJECT

21 Make a **Try New Things** lottery box.

- Write activities on cards.
- Cut a hole in a box.
- Put the cards in the box.
- Choose three activities. Pick one to try!

22 **Complete the sentences with your own information.**

1. My birthday is on ______________________.
2. My favorite kind of music is ______________________.
3. I think riding a bicycle is ______________________.
4. My favorite movie is ______________________.
5. I don't know how to ______________________.
6. There are ______________________ students in my class.
7. I think playing the piano is ______________________.
8. My favorite day of the week is ______________________.

23 **Write your answers from 22 next to the correct numbers in the dialogue. Practice the dialogue with your classmates.**

Troy: Hey, Daniela. Do you know how to [5]______________________?

Daniela: Of course! I [5]__________________ [6]__________________ times a week! Would you like to learn how to do it?

Troy: Yes, I would! But I think it's a little [7]______________________.

Daniela: Well, Troy, some people think that. But I think it's really [3]______________________.

Troy: Well, OK. Can you teach me?

Daniela: Sure! Can you come to my house next [8]______________________?

Troy: Oh, I have to go to my [2]______________________ lesson that day. How about on [1]______________________?

Daniela: Sorry. I'm going to go see [4]______________________ then.

Troy: Oh well, maybe another time.

Daniela: OK, bye!

24 **Read the questions. Write answers.**

1. What does she think of rock music? *(amazing)*

   ____

2. What do they think of speaking Chinese? *(difficult)*

   ____

3. What does he think of watching movies? *(interesting)*

   ____

4. What do you think of playing tennis?

   ____

25 **Read the questions. Write answers with information about yourself.**

1. Which sports do you know how to play?

   ____

2. What songs do you know how to sing?

   ____

3. What kinds of food do you know how to make?

   ____

26 **Complete with information about yourself.**

1. I don't know how to ____________________.
   But ____________________.

2. I'd like to learn how to ____________________.
   I think it's ____________________.

I Can
- [ ] **talk about things people know how to do.**
- [ ] **give opinions.**

Checkpoint | Units 7–9

How Well Do I Know It? Can I Use It?

1 **Read and circle.**

I know this. I need more practice. I don't know this.

	PAGES	I know this.	I need more practice.	I don't know this.
Special days: anniversary, birthday, New Year's Day, Valentine's Day . . .	82–83			
Ways to celebrate: eat special foods, give/get presents, have a party, watch fireworks, watch a parade . . .	82–83			
Hobbies: basketball, chess, coin collection, doll collection, shell collection, soccer . . .	94–95			
Special talents: bake a cake, build a robot, dance hip-hop, draw comic books, speak Chinese . . .	106–107			
When **is** she **going to have** the party? **She** is going to have it **on Monday.** Are you going to visit Pam **on the seventh?** Yes, **on the seventh.** / No, **on the twentieth.**	86–87			
Chris has a **big** stamp collection. Katie's collection is **bigger** than Chris's collection. Kyle has the **biggest** stamp collection. Laura is **a good / a better / the best** dancer. My brother's drawings are **bad / worse / the worst**.	98–99			
Do you **know how to play** the piano? Yes, I do. / No, I don't. What would you **like to learn**? I'd like to **learn how to play** the piano. What **does** she **think of** tennis? She **thinks** it's a lot of fun.	110–111			

I Can Do It!

B43

2 Get ready.

A. Complete the dialogue. Use the words from the box and a form of *be going to*. Then listen and check.

be (2)	dance	do (3)	play	sing

Samuel: Hey, __________ you __________ something for the school talent show on May 9?

Melissa: I don't know. Maybe. Who __________ in it?

Samuel: Well, Caitlyn and Julia __________.

Melissa: Oh, wow. They're better dancers than I am.

Samuel: And Lucas __________.

Melissa: He's the best singer in the class! I need to find something else I can do.

Samuel: Let's see . . . Ricardo __________ skateboard tricks. And Jen __________ the guitar.

Melissa: Hey, I know what I can do!

Samuel: Great. What?

Melissa: I can catch food. Watch! [*Melissa throws up a piece of popcorn and catches it in her mouth.*]

Melissa: __________ anyone else __________ that at the talent show?

Samuel: No, I don't think so.

Melissa: Excellent! I __________ the best food catcher at the show!

B. Practice the dialogue in **A** with a partner. Then practice again. Make up your own answers.

C. Ask and answer the questions with a partner.

1. Why doesn't Melissa want to sing or dance in the talent show?

2. What special talents do you have? Explain.

3 Get set.

STEP 1 Make a poster for a school talent show. First, cut out the strips on page 127.

STEP 2 Glue the strips onto a sheet of paper or poster board.

STEP 3 Design your poster. Add your own pictures and text. Now you're ready to **Go!**

I think Leia's poster is the best one. It has the coolest design!

4 Go!

A. Are you ready? Hang up your posters around the classroom. Look at all the posters and vote on the best one.

B. Make a sign-up sheet for your poster and hang it on the wall. Go around the class and sign up for five other talent shows. Choose a different talent for each one.

Name	Talent
Luisa	sing my favorite song
Celia	say a poem I wrote
Ricky	do magic tricks

C. Compare sign-up sheets with your classmates. Work in a group. Tell the group what people are going to do in your talent show.

Ricky's going to do magic tricks at the talent show!

5 **Write about yourself.**

- What do you usually do on your birthday?
- What do you do on school holidays?
- What are you going to do this weekend?
- What special hobbies or talents do you have?
- Do you like being in talent shows? Why or why not?

All About Me

Date: ____________

____

____

____

____

____

____

How Well Do I Know It Now?

6 **Read and circle.**

A. **Go to page 118. Read and circle again. Use a different color.**

B. **Check (✓).**

☐ I can ask my teacher for help.

☐ I can practice.

7 **Rate this Checkpoint. Check the boxes.**

☐ very easy ☐ easy ☐ hard ☐ very hard | ☐ fun ☐ OK ☐ not fun

1 2 3 4 5 6 7 8 9

My Pen Pal

I'd like to tell you about my pen pal. ________ name is
(His/Her)

________________.
(Name)

________ lives in
(He/She)

________________.
(City, Country)

1

I'd like to visit ________________
(place)

and meet ________________.

________ wants to visit me here
(He/She)

in ________________, too!
(where I live)

4

Cutouts for Page 40, Checkpoint Units 1–3

__________ loves to eat
(Name)

__________ food. __________
(adjective) (His/Her)

favorite dish is __________.
(food)

__________ eats it __________.
(He/She) (how often)

I'd like to try it, too!

2

__________ has
(Name)

__________ hair. __________
(adjective) (His/Her)

hair is __________.
(adjective)

__________ is really
(He/She)

__________.
(adjective)

3

eyes hurt	ate too many potato chips
	have a cold
sore throat	yelled too much at the basketball game
	used the computer too much
stomachache	played too many video games
	allergies while playing outside
sneezing	drank too much soda
	watched too much TV

Cutouts for Page 80, Checkpoint Units 4–6

SCHOOL TALENT SHOW

Wednesday, May 9th

6:00 P.M.–7:30 P.M.

School Auditorium

Vote for the best talent!

Sign up to perform by Friday, May 4.

Young Learners English

Movers

Practice Materials

Sampler

Note to students:
These practice materials will help you prepare for the YLE (Young Learners English) Tests. There are three kinds of practice materials in this sampler: Listening, Reading & Writing, and Speaking.

Good luck!

Listening A

– 5 questions –

B44

Listen and look. There is one example.

Getting Ready for School

Time Susan woke up: 7:30

1 What she's having for breakfast: ____________

2 How she's getting to school: ____________

3 What homework she did for today: ____________

4 What she's doing after school: ____________

5 Her chore for today: ____________

– 5 questions –

B45

Listen and look at the pictures. There is one example.

Tim Emma Frank

Jack Jane Mary

Listening C

– 5 questions –

B46

Listen and look. There is one example.

What is Martin's hobby?

A ☐

B ☐

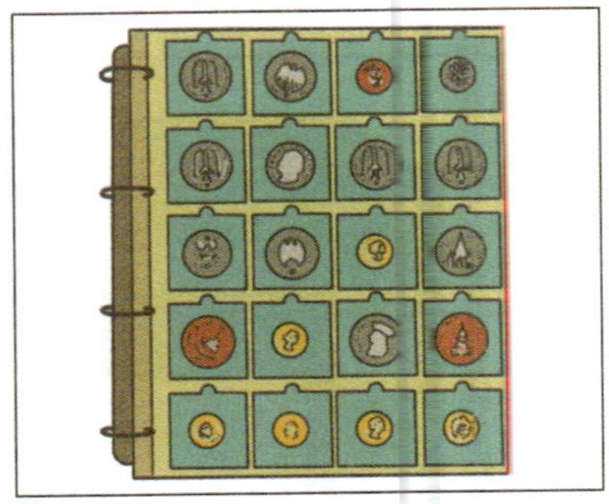

C ☑

1 What does Jane like to do?

A ☐

B ☐

C ☐

2 Which instrument does Anthony know how to play?

A ☐

B ☐

C ☐

3 What is the boy's favorite sport?

A ☐

B ☐

C ☐

4 What is the class going to do?

A ☐

B ☐

C ☐

5 What are they going to do later on?

A ☐

B ☐

C ☐

Reading & Writing A

– 6 questions –

Look and read. Write yes or no.

Examples

The dog knows how to ride a skateboard. ______yes______

The little boy knows how to ride a bicycle. ______no______

Questions

1 The girls know how to play tennis. ________________

2 The man can sing well. ________________

3 The bird knows how to talk. ________________

4 The woman is going to cross the street. ________________

5 A parade is coming. ________________

6 You can see fireworks in the sky. ________________

Reading & Writing B

– 6 questions –

Look and read. Choose the correct words and write them on the lines.

a slide

chess

a guitar

a birthday cake

actors

a comic book

a video game

a robot

Example

This is a game you play on a computer or TV screen. a video game

Questions

1 This is a musical instrument with strings. ______

2 These are the people in a play or movie. ______

3 This is a game you play on a board by moving pieces. ______

4 This is a book that tells a story with pictures and speech balloons. ______

5 This is a machine that does work for people. ______

6 This is something people often eat on their birthdays. ______

Reading & Writing C

– 5 questions –

Read the text and choose the best answer.

Paul is talking to his friend Vicky.

Example

Vicky: Hi, Paul. What are you doing?

Paul: A I'm fine, thank you.
B I had a party.
(C) I'm making a cake.

Questions

1 **Vicky:** What is it for?

Paul: A It's for my parents' anniversary.
B On the last day of the year.
C It's two days until Mother's Day.

2 **Vicky:** Would you like some help?

Paul:
A OK. What time?
B Sure, I would love to.
C That would be great.

3 **Vicky:** What would you like me to do?

Paul:
A You can beat the eggs.
B No thanks, I don't like eggs.
C Two eggs are better than one.

4 **Vicky:** Should I use this bowl?

Paul:
A It's not as big as the other one.
B No, use the bigger one.
C Because I like to do it.

5 **Vicky:** And then what are we going to do?

Paul:
A Mix everything and put it in the oven.
B Flour, eggs, and milk.
C The oven is hot now.

6 **Vicky:** When will it be finished?

Paul:
A Every once in a while.
B In about an hour.
C It lasts a long time.

Speaking A

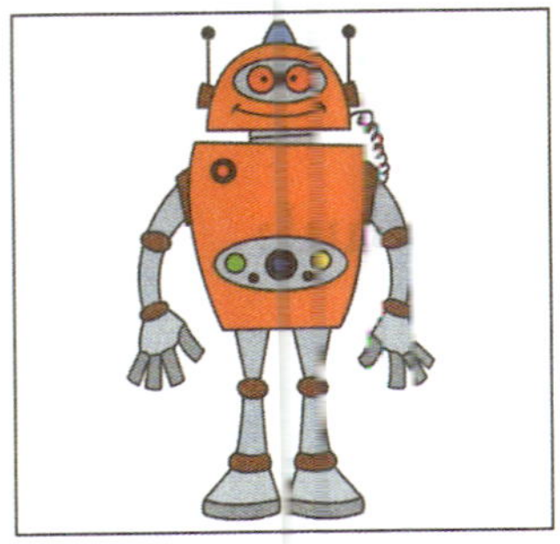

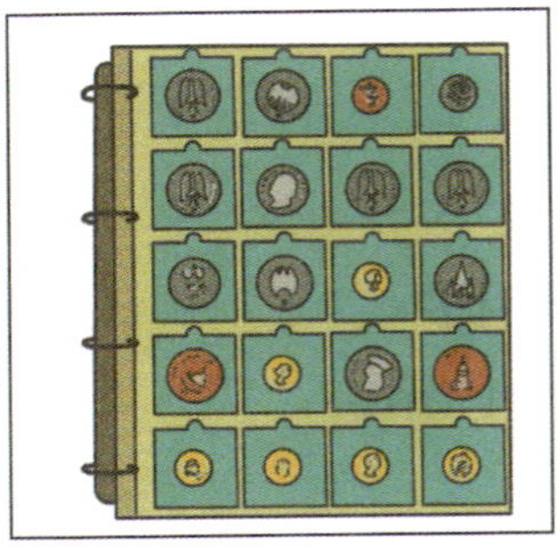

1

2

3

4

Photo credits: Page iii (cr bee) Andrey Armyagov/Shutterstock; 2 (r) KidStock/Getty Images, (l) Amos Morgan/Getty Images, (b) archidea/Shutterstock, (bkgd) lucadp/Shutterstock, (bkgd) Brandon Blinkenberg/Shutterstock; 3 (tl) Fuse/Getty Images, (tc) Stuart Miles/iStockphoto, (cr) karelnoppe/Fotolia, (cl) fotodesign-jegg.de/Fotolia, (c) Kiselev Andrey Valerevich/Shutterstock, (cr) Donskaya Olga/Shutterstock, (bl) Jacek Chabraszewski/Fotolia, (br) Valeriy Lebedev/Fotolia, (bkgd) Brandon Blinkenberg/Shutterstock, (b) archidea/Shutterstock; 6 (tr) imagebroker/Alamy; 7 (br) Monkey Business/Fotolia; 8 (tl) Richard Upshur/iStockphoto, (b) Jaren Jai Wicklund/Shutterstock, (cl) Peter Mintz/Age Fotostock, (bkgd) Jezper/Shutterstock; 9 (cl) Stock Illustrations Ltd/Alamy, (cr) Sara Zinelli/Alamy, (tl) James Boardman/Alamy, (bl) James Boardman/Alamy, (l) Joy Brown/Shutterstock; 11 (tl) Monkey Business Images/Dreamstime, (tr) Rhienna Cutler/iStockphoto, (cl) Ana Abejon/iStockphoto, (cr) Andres Rodriguez/Fotolia, (bl) nami66/Fotolia, (br) chasingmoments/Fotolia; 13 (tr) Blend Images/Fotolia, (tcr) Shchipkova Elena/Shutterstock; 14 (bl) Sonyae/Dreamstime, (br) Radius Images/Glowimages, (bkgd) Racerunner/Dreamstime; 15 (tr) Cathy Melloan/Alamy, (cl) Sean Locke/iStockphoto, (tcr) Chuck Eckert/Alamy, (tl) Scigelova/Dreamstime, (cr) Monkey Business Images/Shutterstock, (bl) Asia Images/SuperStock, (br kids) Blend Images/Alamy, (bkgd corkboard) Devonyu/Dreamstime, (bcr) nami66/Fotolia, (br boy) chasingmoments/Fotolia, (bkgd calendar) Racerunner/Dreamstime, (inset) Kenliu/Dreamstime; 18 (tr) Photo Network/Alamy; 19 (bl) Jacek Chabraszewski/Fotolia; 20 (br) Monkey Business/Fotolia, (c) Olga Lipatova/Shutterstock, (bkgd static) Icefields/Dreamstime; 21 (bkgd) Icefields/Dreamstime; 23 (tl) Spencer Grant/Photo Edit, (tr) Fancy/Alamy, (cl) KidStock/Glowimages, (cr) Jeff Greenough/Glowimages, (bl) nami66/Fotolia, (br) Valeriy Lebedev/Fotolia; 25 (tl) Stock Connection Blue/Alamy, (tc) Juriah Mosin/Shutterstock, (tr) Fotokostic/Shutterstock, (cl) jjpixs/Fotolia, (c) David Page/Alamy, (cr) Monkey Business/Fotolia; 26 (tr) Bramalia/Dreamstime, (bcr) Joe Gough/Fotolia, (l) Juanmonino/iStockphoto, (bkgd) Evlakhov Valeriy/Shutterstock; 27 (tc tacos) Mark Stout/Fotolia, (tr) Juanmonino/iStockphoto, (tcl) Mark Stout Photography/Shutterstock, (cl) Eyewave/Dreamstime, (c) William Mahar/iStockphoto, (cr) Jonathan Downey/iStockphoto, (bl) Franck Boston/Shutterstock, (bcl) Thomas Perkins/Fotolia, (bc) Indigofish/Dreamstime, (bcr) Andy Dean/Fotolia, (br) Rob Marmion/Shutterstock, (tl) fotogal/Fotolia; 30 (t) Monkey Business Images/Shutterstock; 31 (tl) Corbis RF/Alamy, (tcl) Michael Gray/Fotolia, (tcr) Blend Images/Fotolia, (tr) Poonsap/Fotolia, (bl) Julie Eydman/Fotolia, (br) M Itani/Alamy, (bc) Peter zijlstra/Shutterstock; 32 (tr) James Harrop/iStockphoto, (b) Maksim Shmeljov/Shutterstock, (c) USDA/USDA; 33 (tl) Naho Yoshizawa/Glow Images, (tr) bruno ismael da silva alves/Shutterstock, (bl) Ulrich Doering/AgeFotostock, (br) Jörg Beuge/Fotolia, (bkgd tl) Natalia Siverina/Shutterstock, (bkgd tr) Eleonora Kolomiyets/Shutterstock, (bkgd bl) Luba V Nel/Shutterstock, (bkgd br) Malgorzata Kistryn/Shutterstock, (bkgd) Artix Studio/Shutterstock; 34 (c) monticellllo/Fotolia; 35 (br) Monkey Business/Fotolia, (bl) Anna Omelchenko/Fotolia; 36 (b) Yuri Arcurs/Fotolia, (tl) chasingmoments/Fotolia, (tr) Jacek Chabraszewski/Fotolia; 37 (tl) JJAVA/Fotolia, (tc) Artistic Endeavor/Shutterstock, (tr) Paul Johnson/iStockphoto, (bl) Sandra O'Claire/iStockphoto, (bc) CLS Design/Shutterstock, (br) Juanmonino/iStockphoto; 38 (tr) Blend Images/Alamy, (cr) Monkey Business/Fotolia, (bcr) CLS Design/Shutterstock, (br) Radius Images/Glowimages, (bc) monticellllo/fotolia; 41 (bcr) wacpan/Shutterstock, (br) wacpan/Shutterstock; 42 (bl) weestock Images/Alamy (c) BortN66/Shutterstock, (br) karam Miri/Shutterstock, (bkgd) Sura Nualpradid/Shutterstock; 43 (tr) PatrickG/agefotostock, (tcr) Laurent/AGEfotostock, (cr) Maskot/glowImages, (bcr) Palladium/AGEfotoStock, (br) GlowImages/Alamy, (bkgd clipboard) Andrey Eremin/Shutterstock, (bkgd tile) Sura Nualpradid/Shutterstock; 46 (tr) wormdog51/Shutterstock; 47 (bl) Jacek Chabraszewski/Fotolia, (br) Valeriy Lebedev/fotolia; 48 (tl) fusebulb/Shutterstock, (cl) Sebastian Kaulitzki/Shutterstock, (c) nikkytok/Shutterstock, (tcr) Lebendkulturen.de/Shutterstock, (tr) Rudchenko Liliia / Shutterstock, (bkgd) Zhukov/Shutterstock, (br) Ghenadie/Shutterstock; 49 (tl) Kalim/Shutterstock, (cl) Pavel Drozda/Fotolia, (br) strelka/Shutterstock; 51 (bc) Martin Mark Soerensen/AGEfotostock, (bcl) 3445128471/Shutterstock, (b) Yurchyks/Shutterstock, (c) chasingmoments/Fotolia; 53 (cl) Ken Cavanagh / Photo Researchers, Inc, (br) Stiksson/Dreamstime, (cr) Keith Frith/Fotolia, (bl) Gelpi/Dreamstime, (bc) Chassenet/AGEfotostock, (c) Kristy-Anne Glubish I/AGEfotostock; 54 (bl) Corbis Premium RF/Alamy, (tr) Reinhold Föger/Fotolia, (cr) anankkml/Fotolia, (bkgd) Galyna Andrushko/Shutterstock, (br) Chatchawan/Shutterstock, (t) SuriyaPhoto/Shutterstock, (bkgd tr) irin-k/Shutterstock; 55 (tl) America/Alamy, (tc) Gregory MD./Getty Images, (tr) Jon Berkeley/Alamy, (cl) LYNN M. STONE/naturepl.com, (c) The Africa Image Library/Alamy, (cr) haveseen/Fotolia, (bkgd) irin-k/Shutterstock, (br) Ru Bai Le/Shutterstock; 58 (tr) Peter Phipp/Travelshots.com/Alamy; 60 (tl) Lenkadan/Shutterstock, (cr) Godrick/Dreamstime, (bl) Image Source/Fotolia, (cr) Fonetix/Dreamstime; 62 (br) Spaxia/Dreamstime; 63 (tl) TungCheung/Shuttestock, (tc) Kuzma/Shutterstock, (cl) nami66/Fotolia, (cr) chasingmoments/Fotolia, (l) nami66/Shutterstock, (tr) Jerome Whittingham/Shutterstock; 64 (tl) Arco Images GmbH/Alamy, (tc) Images of Africa Photobank/Alamy, (tr) Hadi Djunaedi/Shutterstock, (l) pr2is/Shutterstock, (bl) Monkey Business/Fotolia, (br) Anna Omelchenko/Fotolia, (c) Lukasz Kurbiel/Shutterstock, (cr) shama65/Shutterstock; 65 (c) Marcus Lindström/iStockphoto, (r) Pete Oxford/naturepl.com, (cl) Ronnie Howard/Shutterstock; 66 (b) Yarinca/iStockphoto, (cr) Visions of America, LLC/Alamy, (c) Vadkoz/Dreamstime, (bkgd tr) robynmac/Dreamstime; 67 (tl) Robert Landau/Alamy, (tc) Piotr Marcinski/Shutterstock, (tcr) wavebreakmedia/Shutterstock., (tcl) PhotoAlto/Alamy, (t) Wave/Glow Images, (tr) Lucenet Patrice/Oredia Eurl/SuperStock, (cl) ClassicStock/Alamy, (c) SuperStock/Glow Images, (cr) Vintage Images/Alamy, (bl) GL Archive/Alamy, (bc) Brand Z/Alamy, (br) ClassicStock/Alamy, (bkgd b) Bayanova Svetlana/Shutterstock; 70 (tr) Monkey Business Images /Shutterstock; 72 (tcr) Sam Chadwick/Shutterstock, (cl) Pep Roig/Alamy, (b) Charlie Hutton/Shutterstock, (tr) Kornilovdream/Dreamstime; 73 (tl) Look Die Bildagentur der Fotografen GmbH/Alamy, (bc) dbimages/Alamy, (tr) RIA Novosti/Alamy; 74 (b) Monkey Business/Fotolia; 75 (cl) Anna Omelchenko/Fotolia, (cr) Monkey Business/Fotolia; 76 (tl) Valeriy Lebedev/Fotolia, (tr) Jacek Chabraszewski/Fotolia; 77 (cl) iofoto/Shutterstock, (c) Photononstop/SuperStock, (cr) Marka/SuperStock, (bl) David Davis/Alamy/Shutterstock, (bc) Prisma/SuperStock, (br) Somos/SuperStock; 81 (bcr) wacpan/Shutterstock, (br) wacpan/Shutterstock; 82 (br) Blend Images/Fotolia, (bl) Aldo Murillo/iStockphoto, (bkgd) dpaint/Shutterstock; 83 (tl) Monkey Business/Fotolia, (tc) Blend Images/Alamy, (tr) Miflippo/Dreamstime, (t) Visions of America, LLC/Alamy, (cl) barsik/iStockphoto, (c) Andersen Ross/AgeFotostock, (cr) Monkey Business/Fotolia, (bl) Flowerpower/Fotolia, (bc) elen_studio/Fotolia, (br) Blue Jean Images/Alamy, (tcl) Tetra Images/Alamy, (tcr) Stacy Walsh Rosenstock/Alamy; 86 (tr) iofoto/Fotolia, (tl) iofoto/Fotolia, (tc) Snap2Art/Fotolia; 88 (b) Ruth Black/Fotolia, (br) Dan Burn-Forti/Getty Images; 89 (t) Idris Ahmed/Alamy, (c) Prisma Bildagentur AG/Alamy, (br) Kazuyoshi Nomachi/Corbis, (b) topten22photo/Shutterstock; 91 (tl) Belinda Images/Superstock, (tcl) Charles Register/Alamy, (tcr) BrazilPhotos.com/Alamy, (tr) Francisco Cruz/SuperStock, (cl) Jacek Chabraszewski/Fotolia, (cr) nami66/Fotolia, (bcr) Wdeon/Dreamstime, (b) Contrail/Fotolia, (br) Akiyoko74/Dreamstime; 92 (c) Fancy/Alamy; 93 (tl) Tetra Images/Alamy, (tr) ZUMA Press Inc./Alamy, (bl) David Grossman/Alamy, (br) Blend Images/Alamy; 94 (bl) Corbis Super RF/Alamy; 95 (bcr) Catchlight Visual Services/Alamy, (bcl) Picture Partners/Alamy, (bl) Ian Shaw/Alamy, (br) Michael Newman/Alamy, (border tl) ameli_k/Fotolia, (tl) CJPhoto/Fotolia, (tr) ivan kmit/Fotolia, (border tr) Peter Albrektsen/Shutterstock, (tcl) Louis-Paul St-Onge/iStockphoto, (t) johnrochaphoto/Alamy, (tc) Jacek Chabraszewski/Fotolia, (tcr) AVAVA/Shutterstock, (cl) RF Company/Alamy, (c painter) Anyka/Alamy, (c singer) clearviewstock/Fotolia, (cr) Kamira/Shutterstock, (bkgd br) nami66/Fotolia; 98 (tr) Corbis Flirt/Alamy, (br) Anna Omelchenko/Fotolia; 99 (tl) Igor Plotnikov/Shutterstock, (tc) Jmci/Dreamstime, (tr) Rob Byron/Shutterstock; 100 (cl computer) Gbh007/Dreamstime, (cr) holbox/Shutterstock, (br) Andresr/Shutterstock, (cl kid) image 100/Alamy, (bkgd) Baglieja/Dreamstime; 101 (tl) Jochen Tack/AgeFotostock, (b) HO/AFP/Getty Images/Newscom, (cr) cZUMA Press/Newscom; 103 (cl) Monkey Business/Fotolia, (cr) chasingmoments/Fotolia, (br) Dave King/DK Images; 106 (c) goldenangel/Fotolia, (bkgd) ciarada/Shutterstock; 107 (tl) Alexander Yakovlev/Fotolia, (tcl) Warren Goldswain/Shutterstock, (tcr) Blend Images/Alamy, (tr) goldenangel/Shutterstock, (cl) Peter Weber/Shutterstock, (c) lilufoto/Fotolia, (cr) Konstantin Li/Fotolia, (bl) Stephen Simpson/ZUMA Press/Newscom, (bc) Jeff Greenberg/Alamy, (br) David R. Frazier Photolibrary, Inc./Alamy; 110 (tr) fatihhoca/iStockphoto; 111 (c) Jacek Chabraszewski/Fotolia, (cr) naluwan/Shutterstock, (cl) Gabbro/Alamy, (bl) Anna Omelchenko/Fotolia, (br) Monkey Business/Fotolia; 112 (cr) YorkBerlin/Shutterstock; 113 (border tr) Stuart Tannehill/REUTERS/Newscom, (br) Splash/Newscom, (cr) Alex Hofford/EPA/Newscom; 115 (cl) chasingmoments/Fotolia, (cr) Jacek Chabraszewski/Fotolia; 117 Nejc Vesel/Shutterstock; 118 (tr) Blend Images/Alamy, (cr) flowerpower/Fotolia, (bcr) Peter Albrektsen/Shutterstock, (br) goldenangel/Fotolia, (bc) Visions of America, LLC/Alamy; 120 (tr) irina86roibu/Fotolia; 121 (bcr) wacpan/Shutterstock, (br) wacpan/Shutterstock